The Money Book
for Creative People

THE
AFFLUENT
ARTIST™

How Creative
Could You Be
if Money
Wasn't an Issue?

Rick DiBiasio, CFP®

MORGAN JAMES PUBLISHING • NEW YORK

THE AFFLUENT ARTIST ™

ISBN: 978-1-60037-478-4 (Paperback)
Library of Congress Control Number: 2008936941

Published by:

MORGAN · JAMES ™
THE ENTREPRENEURIAL PUBLISHER
www.morganjamespublishing.com

Morgan James Publishing, LLC
1225 Franklin Ave Suite 325
Garden City, NY 11530-1693
Toll Free 800-485-4943
www.MorganJamesPublishing.com

Cover/Interior Design by:
Rachel Lopez
rachel@r2cdesign.com

Habitat
for Humanity®
Peninsula
Building Partner

PRAISE FOR
THE AFFLUENT ARTIST™

"Most people don't believe they can live their passion and make a lot of money at the same time. Not only does Rick's book debunk that myth, he teaches you HOW to do it. If you want to make a lot of money doing what you love to do, GET THIS BOOK and read it cover to cover so you can LIVE YOUR LIFE OUT LOUD."

SEAN SMITH, *Master Results Coach*
www.BreakthroughToGreatnessNow.com

"Using the art of practical spirituality, true stories and profound financial advice, *The Affluent Artist*™ is a 'must read' for the creative person who wants to implement their creative power to obtain lasting financial abundance, freedom and independence."

LINDA MACKENZIE, *author of "Help Yourself Heal with Self-Hypnosis",
President of Creative Health & Spirit, and Founder of
HealthyLife.Net-All Positive Talk Radio*

The Affluent Artist™ provides a powerful bridge between success as we measure it in money, and fulfillment as we measure it in the sheer joy of creative expression.

SHAYLA ROBERTS, *Entrepreneurial Coach, author, and musician*

For too long now, the terms "starving" and "artist" have been linked in the collective consciousness. Rick Dibiasio is out to change that! In his new book, ***The Affluent Artist***™, Rick has uncovered a key discovery that will keep your artistic bank-account flourishing: the power that allows creativity to flow can also allow abundance to grow! If you are an artist who chooses affluence instead of poverty, don't just read Rick's book, savor it–it was written just for you! Now is the time to start upon your journey toward true wealth!

PAM GARCY, *PhD*
The Power of Inner Guidance: Seven Steps to Tune In and Turn On
http://www.myinnerguide.com

Rick DiBiasio has written an incredible book that will help not only creatives, but will help all of us who believe we do have an artist within, and yet lack the financial acumen to build our financial foundation that will allow us to release the brakes, so we can do the creative work we know we are meant to do. The Affluent Artist™ is destined to help many reach these goals.

BARBARA KOFFSKE REID, *Director Bachelor Science in Human Services, Cambridge College and emerging artist!*

Rick DiBiasio's new book "The Affluent Artist™" is not only timely but really hitting the spot with many, many people. The old saying "do what you love and the money will follow" is not just a saying but a reality for more and more of us. With overall job satisfaction in corporate America seeming to be at a low point, people are searching for ways to fill their soul and their pocketbook at the same time. With the proper understanding of the Law of Attraction, it is not only possible to turn any form of creativity into a money making business it's universal law. I personally walked away from a lucrative job in sales and turned my love for animals, into a wonderful business helping thousands and soon to me millions of people and their dogs. My heart sings everyday, if I am having a rough day or I'm not in a particularly good mood, I go to work! Rick DiBiasio is a shining light for those who are looking to turn their passion into their career.

BRAD JAFFE *Team Canine, Inc.*
www.teamcanine.com
www.conversationswithcourtney.com

This book is a blessing for creative people who want to achieve more financially and professionally. It is also a true gift for people who are already experiencing financial success AND feel a desire let out more of their creative side. In *The Affluent Artist*™, Rick DiBiasio shows us that it is possible to be both wealthy and creative/artistic, without sacrificing what you love about your life now. The information and strategies that Rick shares in this book are working to create remarkable lives for him and his clients and they can work for you too!"

ROBERT MACPHEE *Heart Set, Inc.*
P.O. Box 232155, Encinitas, CA 92023
(760) 632-4909
www.heartset.com

Finally a book that marries money and art. Most people stick their head in the sand when it comes to finances, especially artists. They think that you have to suffer to create art. I highly disagree. I believe creativity is a gift and there's no need to starve. Rick inspires me because he's creating a paradigm shift in the way artists perceive themselves. He's giving tools of self-empowerment that allow you to be creative and successful. Starving Artist no more, bring on the Affluent Artist™!

JOANNA GARZILLI, *America's Intuition Coach*™
http://www.joannagarzilli.com

DEDICATION

Watch My Back and Light My Way
My Traveling Star

-JAMES TAYLOR

To My Creative Stars
Thank You for Your Inspiration

I Hope Your Work Makes Your Soul Happy!

TABLE OF CONTENTS

FOREWORD

BY JACK *Canfield*

One of the great universal truths is that when the student is ready the teacher will appear. I know that you have picked up this book because you are now ready to be taught how to welcome more abundance and prosperity (including money) into your life.

The teacher you have chosen, Rick DiBiasio CFP®, and I met when he attended my Breakthrough to Success Training and later became a member of my Platinum Inner Circle Coaching Program. I have come to know Rick as a sincere, caring individual with a knack for making complicated financial concepts easy to understand and even fun to read about. Rick has a passion for helping others become successful, and this book evolved from his experience with the other wonderful souls in my programs—many of whom are artists, writers, and musicians.

Rick has brilliantly married many of the principles I teach on the law of attraction and manifesting success with his vast knowledge and experience as a financial planner, resulting in a fabulous book that will help you achieve and maintain much more abundance and prosperity in your life. Rick has applied these principles in his own life and has achieved much greater success in every area of his life. The same is possible for you. Rick teaches from his experience. He has lived what he is teaching in this book and has proven that these principles work, and now he is sharing them with you.

I know from my experience working with Rick over the past year that this book is a labor of love. Rick has a genuine passion for helping others, and this book is his way of expressing how much he has to offer and how much he wants to help you. As you will see very quickly in the pages ahead, Rick has an incredibly in-depth knowledge about the financial world. This knowledge combined with his passion for contributing is what makes this book such a gift to anyone who wants to do the work they love *and* improve their financial situation at the same time.

As the father of three sons—all of whom are artists, musicians and writers— I know how challenging it can be to make a living while pursuing your art. In fact, at one time in my family, we had a standing joke that went like this:

Question: What do you call a musician without a girlfriend?

Answer: Homeless!

While it is funny, it is all too often true. I have had hundreds of students and clients who were artists and musicians, sculptors and photographers, children's book writers and illustrators, poets and screenwriters, and all too often they were struggling financially for way too long in their careers. The phrase "starving artist" is familiar to everyone, because too often, and totally unnecessarily, artists are just that—starving, struggling to pay the rent, unable to support the pursuit of their art with all the raw materials and the free time they need to let their creativity take full flight. We all know an artist working in a retail store when she should be working in her studio, the screenwriter and actor that is waiting tables in Beverly Hills, the gifted musician who is deejaying someone's fifteenth birthday party instead of playing his own music.

Whether your creative side is currently hidden behind your "day job," or you are already in a position where you are able to express your creativity in your job or with a significant portion of your discretionary time, *The Affluent Artist*, will inspire you to bring out more of your creativity and express it for your own enjoyment and the benefit of others. It will also help you understand how to generate more income with your talent and how to set yourself up for a secure financial future.

Most people in the world, not just artists, have had had no prior training or experience in consciously managing their money. When they do earn more, they are unaware of how to manage it, protect it and grow it. They are, for lack of a better term, financially illiterate. Rick will help you become financially literate so that you will always have all the money you need to live the life of your dreams.

Another thing I have noticed in working with tens of thousands of people in my seminars over the last 30 years is that the "creatives"—the artists—are usually the people who are more likely to want to change the world. They can see the hypocrisies, the self-delusions, the cultural trances, and the inconsistencies in the world more clearly than the rest of us. And most artists want to express this in some way. They want to have an impact on people. They want to make a difference. They want to wake us up, make us see what they see, hear what they hear, feel what they feel.

Many artists also use their art to help raise funds for causes they care deeply about ranging from the displaced victims of attempted genocide in Darfur or the victims of natural disasters such as Hurricane Katrina to the AIDS victims in Africa and the suffering of abused children in the United States. They often use their art form to communicate messages for those without a voice—the prisoners, the homeless, the abused, the ignored, the disenfranchised, the forgotten.

Obviously, not all art is intended to have a deep social message, but artists seem to be more sensitive to these issues than many other professions. The tragedy is that those with the greatest insight into what is not working and often the greatest desire to help, are often not able to contribute as much as they would like due to a lack of funds. One of the things I learned early on in my career is that without money, the good you can do in the world is limited to what you can do in one place at one time with your physical presence. With money, you can contribute to projects all over the world at the same time. So…if you are one of those people who want to make a big difference in the world, money will help you to do that.

As you will discover in the pages ahead, Rick is passionate about creating a new Renaissance, passionate about helping creative people achieve financial independence so they can sponsor or joint venture with other creative people. Imagine the power of a group of financially independent authors, artists and entrepreneurs, united to change the world. There is no limit to the problems that could be solved, to the people that could be saved, to the new creations that would spring forth.

The Affluent Artist is your invitation and your road map to attract and allow more money into your life, to embrace the basics of financial planning and to experience the freedom that comes with financial independence.

Read, underline and study this book. Then apply the principles and strategies that Rick offers here. If you do, your life will become all you want it to be—perhaps even more than you ever imagined it could be. Don't settle for anything less! You deserve to have it all. It is time to claim it!

JACK CANFIELD
Featured teacher in The Secret, co-author of *Chicken Soup for the Soul*, *The Success Principles*™ and *Jack Canfield's Key to Living the Law of Attraction*

INTRODUCTION

When word of my project, *The Affluent Artist*™, began to get out, artists seemed to come looking for me—someone I'd interviewed would call and ask if I'd talk to a creative friend, or a new client (who just happened to be an artist) would show up in my office. One day—at a time when I was wondering if my message to creative people was getting lost in all of the financial stuff—Sue Thompson wandered in. She'd heard me give a talk called "If Everyone Cared" at our Rotary Club, part of a program I lead for educators in urban schools to help build self-esteem in students. It would have been a great day just for having a chance to get to know Sue, but later that night that I would realize why a financial planning guide for artists was such a necessary tool.

Sue is a public artist of note in Central Florida, primarily known as a sculptor; she is also a photographer, writer, and painter. As the daughter of migrant workers, Sue grew up following the harvest all over America, moving from camp to camp. She saw more than anyone's share of violence and hardship, but she remembers that there was always someone who cared enough to make sure she got a rudimentary education. She always had the strength to believe in herself; without it she would not be the successful artist she is today.

When she finally took a GED exam at 19 and entered the University of Central Florida as an art major—the first time in her life that she would live in one place for more than a few months—she remembers feeling like she was in a "prison cell." She found it hard to relate to students who complained how hard school was. "They just need *one* summer in the fields . . ." Her background, instead of crippling her, was a source of strength: "I've already been poor; I knew how to be poor. There was no place for me to go but up!" Sue understood the value of her college education and worked hard—she knew no other way.

Sue's education and her work as an artist has enabled her to travel the world, open her own studio, and mentor young artists. While dealing with her own cancer, she lost her Mother and sister to the disease and today helps care for her Grandson, an aspiring actor, and her wonderful Granddaughter, who is stricken with cerebral palsy. When a local developer wanted to honor the history of our community in a new shopping plaza, Sue was the most logical choice to create the statues and plaques along the "History Walk."   The centerpiece of the exhibit is a statue of an enchanting young girl, on an orange crate in the center of a beautiful fountain; she is a beacon of hope for our community's future and also honors our past. If you look closely, you'll see that her legs are not quite straight, that she might be having a little trouble standing. Yes, she is Sue's granddaughter, the one with cerebral palsy. The committee picked her for the plaza's centerpiece without knowing who she was or how she was related to the artist. You can be sure that no one in history *ever* created a work of art with more love and passion.

On the evening of the day that I met Sue, I served "board duty" at the Little League field. I was there to make sure the games were going smoothly and that the concession stand wasn't on fire. It was the kind of Central Florida night that you move here for, mid seventies, a full moon and we were surrounded by six fields of kids playing baseball (God, I hope heaven is like this). On duty with me was my friend Darren, a Certified Financial Analyst and mutual fund manager. In my office (I am a Certified Financial Planner™) I interact with clients and recommend appropriate investments. Darren is the guy who actually calls corporate finance officers and asks them all kinds of questions about their business and their balance sheets—he will either buy or sell stocks in his firm's portfolio, based on the answers he gets. He doesn't really interact with clients. He manages the money that is sent to his firm on behalf of clients. Darren loves numbers, spreadsheets, financial statements and his computer. He's a great guy, a good Dad, a baseball fan, and he has a promising career ahead of him.

Darren and I were sitting on a park bench and as long as the conversation stayed on baseball or investments, he was fully engaged. Twice I mentioned my book, and twice he got up to check the games or the hotdogs. Darren's Wall Street orientation just wouldn't allow him to get his arms around things like doing business from a perspective of love and abundance, the genesis of artistic creation, a new Renaissance, or any of the other touchy feely things I was writing about in *The Affluent Artist™*. Before long I felt a little silly and got up to make sure the hotdogs weren't burning too.

That night I woke up from a sound sleep and realized that my day had been a metaphor for my book. Sue, who prides herself in being analytical and in having a good business sense, would not use the same language to talk about money that Darren does. Like many of the artists I talked with, she is very bright; she knows how to run her business, but an education in finance isn't something she has had to acquire. She hasn't had to learn to speak the language of investments and Darren, I'm guessing, doesn't know a lot about creating statues.

I interviewed all kinds of creative people in researching this book; in fact, I finally started telling artists who wanted to talk with me that I'd have to talk with them for my *next* book. Without exception, the historic stereotype of the starving artist is something they resent. Money is usually something they just haven't gotten around to dealing with. After a while, I had met so many people who call themselves creative that I wondered if everyone has a frustrated artist hiding inside. I aim this discussion at professional creatives, people who are under the gun to make a living from their creative passion, including those who wait tables while building an artistic career.

Another thing all of the creative people I talked with shared was that they attribute the source of their creativity to a higher power. They explained having words, music or art come to them from a place they couldn't explain. Some called it God, some the Universe, and others didn't quite have a name for it. Eventually I came to the conclusion that, whatever you call this source, it is also what provides financial opportunity. I believe that artists are as likely to gain financial success as anyone else in America is. After all, this is still called the land of opportunity! Capitalizing on it requires being open to the concept of financial success, getting a little education, and taking action. Action, by the way, is the most important step: you can believe you are going to win the lottery, know you are going to win the lottery, but your chances of winning the lottery actually improve slightly if you buy a lottery ticket!

So, this book is for Sue and other creative people like her. I didn't write a purely financial book—you'd have read one by now if you had wanted to. No, this is an invitation to money and abundance. I'm acting as your interpreter, just as I would if Sue and my friend Darren were going to talk about investing. *The Affluent Artist*™ is an invitation to stop starving if you are a starving artist. It's an invitation to the Corporate Creative to keep in touch with his inner artist, to the self-employed artist to keep creating while running a business, and to the Affluent Artist™ to continue to grow financially. *It's an invitation to make money your ally and to achieve artistic independence by achieving financial independence!*

Now, let's face a very important fact right here. Right up front, you probably know a lot of people without any savings. There is a lot of that going around, and it is certainly not restricted to artists. I am never surprised when I meet someone who has no savings and who is living paycheck to paycheck. I know many people who will never have the financial resources to retire or even approach what we call financial independence. Many of these people drive nice cars, live in nice neighborhoods, and take expensive vacations. They are very good at living an affluent lifestyle but not very good with money. They do it all on credit. It's a dirty little secret that many Americans hide behind while driving their Hummers.

As you begin to learn about taking care of your money you'll probably run into a lot of people who scoff at the idea of willing yourself to financial independence. Let me pull rank on them here, just this once: I've been in the financial services industry for a quarter of a century and I have met many affluent people. They don't fit into stereotypes any more than creative people do! I've known doctors without a dime to their names. I've seen people squander inheritances faster than the speed of sound. I've also met plenty of people who would never even think of touching their nest-egg, and I know schoolteachers who literally saved a million dollars. I have no doubt that attaining financial independence requires a mindset, a purpose, and motivation. If you are a creative person, you already know a lot about focus and about motivation. This book is about getting you to use that focus to become financially independent. I know it can be done—I've seen it happen.

The personal finance principles in *The Affluent Artist*™ are beyond simplified (Darren won't be reading them). They are designed to give you some basic concepts and point out some pitfalls that I've noticed in over forty years as an investor and twenty-five as a financial services professional. Creative people *are* different and my hope is that these words might help you to get a handle on finance; to realize that you can create wealth just as you create art; and that your talent and affluence are not mutually exclusive. You can help lead a new Renaissance! Let's get started—are you feeling passionate?

PART 1: Creative Finance

PASSIONATE PEOPLE

CHAPTER 1: *Passion!* As I interviewed creative people from all over America, I kept coming back to this word. Passion is what drives you, it fuels creativity. Passion makes you get up and strum a new melody into a tape recorder at midnight or play in a pool with dolphins when it's too cold for any sensible person to swim. It's the very essence of a creative person. No matter what your art form, your profession, or your success level, you are passionate. One creative person I know just refers to all creatives as *passionate people* and after all of my research, I can't come up with a better description. In a world where most people are content to get a paycheck, benefits, and vacation, you are passionate about your work and that makes all of the difference.

It's hard to imagine the toll-taker on the highway, the clerk at the convenience store or the guy selling cars as passionate about their work, isn't it? Are they passionate about something else? Do they just have a nine-to-five to support their real passion or is life just passing them by? The more I talked with creative people, the more I wondered what sets them apart. Why live life on the road less chosen—what compels someone to identify himself as a creative person? Even in writing this book, I read all the articles that told me not to expect to earn any money as an author, talked with consultants who told me it wouldn't help my financial planning practice, and dealt with the fear that accompanies putting your deepest thoughts out there to be judged by others. But you know what? This book was in me and it had to come out. I literally couldn't help but write it. In short, I am passionate about the people that I help and about the things I want to tell you!

THE CREATIVE CLASS

Have you been told all of your life that you are creative? Have you always liked to color outside the lines? Are you lucky enough to have a job that relies on your imagination? Or do you wish you could have a job like that? Is there an inner artist in you desperately trying to escape? Is he making you crazy? Have you tried to leave art alone, to be more "normal" but you just keep coming back to it? You are not alone, and I'm happy that I found you!

As we emerge from a manufacturing economy to one that is information-based, the number of people who are paid for their vision, their wit, and their artistic ability is growing. Richard Florida, in his book *The Rise of the Creative Class*, says that over thirty percent of the U.S. work force can now be defined as creative. Some of these people are fulfilled and happy, almost too busy and excited about their jobs to worry about mundane things like personal finance. Others are frustrated because the constraints of their employment are holding back their creativity. They live for the day when they can express themselves fully and without compromise. Somehow life has gotten between them and their creative process, and money poses a question they can't answer.

Traditional artists—people like painters, songwriters, actors, and authors—are no longer out of the mainstream. A person who is designing a video game based on a movie is just as creative as the person who wrote the movie and as the person who acted in it. That cultural phenomenon, "the starving artist", isn't so common or even fascinating anymore, thanks to the Internet and technology. Creative people are finding all kinds of ways to become wealthy. Those that have not become wealthy have more opportunity to get paid for their art than ever before.

"Painting is easy. The hard part is
paying for the frame."

CREATE NOW, PAY LATER

In my experience, many creative people have problems with their money. I don't mean they are broke, at least not all of them. I don't mean they are incapable. They definitely are intelligent and quick to catch on to things. For a variety of reasons, however, many creative people either don't care about money or don't want to deal with it. In our credit card, buy it now-pay for it years later, consumer-driven society, personal finance is not a subject that people like to dwell on. For many people whose passions are centered on their art, money is just one of those things to worry about some other time.

I wrote this book because I am fascinated by the creative process and by the amazing people who are driven by their own creativity. I love those people who color outside the lines with their lives, those people who call themselves artists. Maybe they don't all paint, or act, or sing—maybe they are hair stylists or graphic artists—but the point is something inside them has to come out. They just can't help it! These people would no sooner stop creating than stop breathing. I admire their talent, their enthusiasm and their passion. If you find someone who has liberated her inner artist, you find someone who is interesting to have in your life and an inspiration too!

WITH RESPECT

Often when you meet a truly creative person, the combination of energy and enthusiasm that bubbles up from within is infectious. As a very bad guitar picker, I envy the truly creative. I got the "good with money gene," you got the fun genes. At least I get to listen to your music while I do a financial plan. Thank God we are there for each other!

As I work with talented people like you, I've come to respect your fragility. I know how hard it is to put yourself out there and possibly have your creation rejected! It is awful to be told that something you transmitted through your soul is not acceptable because of commercial considerations. It takes courage (or at least innocence and naiveté) to put your creation out there and hope it doesn't get shoved back in your face.

The excess we often attribute to artists is this fragility brought to life. Your creative existence often depends upon the subjective whims of others. Somehow, we have come to think of the "true artist" as someone who doesn't care what other people think. They are satisfied with the purity of their creation and don't care if they find an audience. This great conflict between artistic integrity and finding a market for your art is a powerful dynamic. Is it any wonder that creative people can be a little eccentric? I appreciate your fears.

What if your gift has an expiration date? Dancers, like all athletes, know that their bodies will only hold up for so long. Writers worry, "What if this is the only book that ever comes to me?" Actresses, how long can you play an ingénue? And for all of you, what if you are only given the gift temporarily? How many bands were one hit wonders? How many painters became famous only after they died? And, "What if the world changes and I become yesterday's style? Please, God, don't let me end up singing at dinner theater in Daytona Beach!" (Dinner theater in Daytona Beach is probably a perfectly lovely experience. Try the veal—it's the best in town!)

And then, there's the whole question of abundance: I believe your gift is limitless and you can have every material possession that you desire. I believe the Universe is at your disposal. You just have to be open to possibility and the Law of Attraction. In interviewing my artists, almost without exception, I found that they attribute their source of inspiration to something or someone beyond themselves. Whether it is God, the Universe, or whatever, few artists take credit for their creativity. My belief is that the same source that you draw from creativity from is also available to you financially. No matter what your experience has been, no matter what your well-meaning friends tell you, be open to the possibility, as you read this book, that you can attract wealth into your life.

Where are you on this issue? Has money been there when you've needed it in the past? The theme of this book, really, is Financial Independence. It's about *getting to a point where your money can take care of you because you have taken care of your money* and I believe that anyone can reach this point. So: why not you?

If you believe in abundance, if you believe you can achieve financial independence, these are some questions you should have about money and I want to answer some of them: "How do I know enough, just enough, to know that people are not taking advantage of me and my money? What good could I do if I wrote that bestseller? Who could I help if my script is picked up by a Hollywood?" And here's the big one— here's the question that I believe every single creative person needs to ask:

"HOW CREATIVE COULD I BE IF MONEY WASN'T AN ISSUE?"

I am a Certified Financial Planner™ and in my almost twenty-five years in the financial services industry, I've developed a niche working with people who consider themselves creative. It's a lot of fun. I never really know what fascinating person will come into my life next. It might be a dance teacher, an animal trainer, a Broadway actress, or the creator of a national line of hair care products. Someone (or something) has sent them to me for help with their personal finances because they know I speak English (not the Wall Street version) and that I can make all of this money stuff a little easier to digest. It's that approachability that I want to bring to you here. I want to lift some of the fog that surrounds money and invite you to the party. Oh yeah, I am pretty much a smartass, and I'll make you laugh any chance I get. Sometimes I'll be very absurd in my examples— my kids hate this—but I'm writing the anti-Wall Street financial book for you, and playfulness is not plentiful in the financial community. It's okay if you think I'm not that funny, I'm used to that. I've raised four kids who tell me how un-funny I am all the time (sigh).

DON'T KNOW MUCH ABOUT HISTORY

As I said, Americans in general are not real good at personal finance: more than sixty-seven percent of adults, in a recent survey, admitted they are not saving enough for retirement. Obviously money worries are not limited to creative people, but I've always wondered why a person who can memorize five minutes of complex dance steps with very little explanation has trouble balancing a checkbook. And I wonder why a person who can produce a successful Broadway show can demonstrate little or no interest in saving for retirement. I wonder how someone who never concentrated on anything but their art can be expected to become a financial genius suddenly when they hit it big. There is no preparation for some of the things that come along with fame and fortune! If you just wrote a hit record and have spent your life at the piano, how are you supposed to know about estimated tax payments, retirement plans, stocks, bonds or any of the other nine thousand things that are suddenly concerns when you get your first royalty check?

Our schools do a terrible job of teaching us anything about money and success. You might cover American and European history a half a dozen times in your schooling, but I bet you never had a course that made finance come alive for you, one that alerted you to the wonderful possibilities that await you if you take care of your money. Our textbooks are rooted in the great depression: money is evil or it's something that's not to be discussed in polite society! Somehow we get the message that money and finance are something other people need to know, not us! In the greatest economy in the history of the world, no one gives us the message that we can have it all, that abundance is ours for the asking, that financial success is something we should expect and go after!

WHAT'S WITH CREATIVITY?

At some point I wondered how the whole creative thing works, so I began to do some research and ask some questions. What is that particular combination of inspiration, ego, and talent that tells somebody to just go with the feeling, to trust that what they have to express is so good that other people must see it? I wondered if some people were just so overly blessed and endowed in one area that the mere details concerning other aspects of life were beyond them. That didn't turn out to be true. In my research, I met plenty of creative people who were just fine at managing money and other details of life. They make good livings and have normal families, live in suburbia and barbecue out by the pool alongside their neighbors with normal jobs. The difference: they get to go to work and create really cool stuff! I don't think that the concept of managing money is beyond people who are creative. I believe it is a matter of choice.

I wondered about that whole starving artist thing. What if your particular creativity doesn't result in something that is marketable? One busy message board for creatives featured the topic "I'm finally free to create but no one wants to buy my art!" If you do find someone to buy your art or to pay you to create something, how do you feel about money during that process? Is your integrity somehow challenged? Or does money motivate you? Does it help you to create on an even higher level? There is no consensus here, either: I've talked with people who freeze the minute someone wants to buy their work and others who prefer only to create when there is a paycheck at hand.

Some of the creative people I know are just consumed by their work and the creative process. Their passion does not have a volume dial. (I don't mean in a crazy way, they aren't lopping off their own ears!) They are what the rest of us would call really, really busy, always thinking about work when they are at home and always coming up with new ideas and improvements for their projects. They are so into their work and so caught up in the next task that trivial things such as paychecks, 401(k)s, and benefits are something to be dealt with later. Always later! I envy these people in a lot of ways. They get to play in the sandbox, never coming out to be with the adults. For many of them, a loving life partner is there to take care of life's small details, like money, but for others the real world of finance is something they never get around to dealing with.

AND YOU?

What about you? How do you feel about money? Do you attract it when you most need it? Do you think that whole power of attraction thing works for you? Maybe you have an inner artist, an artist who is dying to break out but who just can't do it right now because of money concerns. Are you waiting tables or working for a big corporation? Are you allowed to be somewhat creative, within the context of the company's needs, but feeling like the creative voice within you is screaming to come out?

Maybe, you've made it. Maybe you have written a best-selling book, or your design company has just gone public, or people actually pay to hear you sing! But you still wonder about all this financial stuff and whether the people you hired to help you are doing a good job. That's natural: the difference between a financial planner and an opera star is pretty dramatic. There are gifts, personality traits, and training that go into mastering either. It's pretty hard to be good at both. (If you need further proof, I will now sing from The Barber of Seville while Bernardo, the tenor, does my taxes.)

YOUR HALL PASS

This book is your hall pass—you can wander all over the financial campus with it and ask whatever you've been afraid to bring up about money. You may only vaguely know the difference between a stock and bond. Your pass will allow you to skip around hearing different lectures, even if you suspect this thing called saving money is only a rumor and that income taxes are a problem that you only wish you had! It's okay, you are safe on this campus. Be curious—you can even be creative—we appreciate you being here. We are going to do everything we can to help you be more successful. We'll help you construct a financial foundation that you can build on for the rest of your life. If you haven't paid a lot of attention to money or to investing and you really don't want to start now, that's OK, you get a hall pass, too!

I'm going to ease you through the process. I'm going to tell you why it's OK to be friendly with your money (You don't have to love it, but you do need to be on speaking terms!). I'm going to tell you how and when to ask someone for help (and when not to). I'm going to give you permission to get past the whole starving artist thing. You will no longer have to feel like a tortured soul who is selling out if you're getting paid to pass your creativity on to others. At the very least I hope my experience and some of my stories will stir an interest in personal finance and let you know that there are others out there just like you!

There are, in fact, people in the financial community who love you and who appreciate you. Some of us would much rather be in a room full of creative people than one full of bankers. We would rather be reading your novel than a prospectus, and we would want to see you become financially independent so you can create even more for our enjoyment. Your energy and enthusiasm, and yes, even your passion, is America's number one export. There is already a marriage between you and the world economy. People are literally reaping fortunes from your work and your passion is driving the world. I want you to get your share—you deserve it! So let's talk a little more about this person we call "Creative"…

CREATIVE PEOPLE ARE DIFFERENT

CHAPTER 2: To some extent, all human beings are creative but the person who is labeled as creative early on is someone who has been identified as a person who doesn't quite fit the mold. The accountant sees numbers and applies things he has learned, like tax law, to them. A craftsman takes a set of plans and builds a house or a piece of furniture according to the specifications in the plan. But a creative person sees something that *isn't* there and makes it happen. It's a "vision thing" to quote a former president. The creative person has the confidence to see his vision through to fruition. More than just a technical skill like carpentry or house painting, the artist puts herself in her work. It's the difference between someone who can type and a poet. This personality type that we call creative has been studied by psychologists, and it turns out you might be wired just a little differently than the rest of us.

I've asked artists about the decision to go with their art, to follow their bliss, and almost all of them feel they have no choice. They could no sooner turn off their creativity than they could stop breathing. While some creative people seek to change their appearance and to adopt an attitude that lets the world know they are artists, other very creative people live next door, have 2.3 kids, drive a mini van, and are somewhat corporate in demeanor. Even the category creative is a tough one to get a handle on. Besides your stereotypical artist types, there are scientists, computer designers and countless other people who consider themselves to be creative. Okay, artist is a pretty broad term too. In fact, since *one third of our population is now considered creative*, we'll have to just go with a loose definition. You can decide if it resonates with you.

DO YOU BREAK CRAYONS?

Let's talk about some of the traits that you may have as a creative person and why they may inhibit you when it comes to money. It seems that some of your wiring might just be a little different and it might actually be against your nature to worry about (or even like) money. Yes, people are different, and yes, some people are more predisposed to excel at some things than others. Recent psychological studies have indicated that some of the things that allow you to be more creative are some of the things that make you hate reading the *Wall Street Journal*!

Robert Alan Black, a noted psychologist and author of *Breaking Crayons* has dedicated his career to studying people like you and helping you to excel in your field. He has identified the following attributes of creative people (in bold face) and, where appropriate, I've added some reasons that money might be an issue (or non-issue):

Sensitive: Artists are open to the Universe and the possibility of creative inspiration being behind every closed door.

Not Motivated by Money: *Yes, I know. You are motivated by creation. We are hoping to help you see that money can be a tool, not a barrier.*

Sense of Destiny: Creative people know they have a purpose because of their skill or talent. Money is an after thought. They believe, strongly, that the importance of their work is reason enough for the work. Money is neither a block nor a motivation.

Adaptable: You adapt to things that suit you. You can live in a crappy apartment and drive an old car. You will adapt to your surroundings as long as your art is allowed to come forth.

Tolerant of ambiguity: You see things from many different perspectives. Your lifestyle, your creativity, your view of others is tolerant of contradiction. You understand both sides of most arguments.

Observant: Creatives are constantly using their senses. The fact that you can identify a certain item in a roomful of objects or hear a dialect in a room full of conversations is one of the things that make you an artist.

Perceive the world differently: Different perspectives open up the world to different possibilities. Oddly, this is a trait that you share with great investors. We'll talk more later about being a "contrarian." This is a really cool trait to have when it comes to investing!

See Possibilities: Creative people love to see many, even infinite possibilities in most situations or challenges. *May I be so humble as* *to suggest that if you include your own financial independence as one of those possibilities, you are onto something!*

Question Asker: It is in your nature to question. This is a great trait for an artist *and an investor.*

You can grasp the whole picture with only a few pieces, even with the major pieces missing. You are intuitive, and I envy you. I can't look at blueprints and visualize the house. You probably see it in color!

Able to Fantasize: People have always told you to stop looking out the window and pay attention in class. *How about fantasizing about being financially independent for a while?*

Flexible: Creatives are flexible when playing with ideas *(So are good investors.)*

Fluent: A brick can be a brick, but creative might look at a brick as a doorstop, a weapon or a number of things besides what it is intended to be used for. This fluency is a valuable tool for the creative (and the investor).

Original: A driving force for creative people, you also don't have to stop being creative when it comes to motivating yourself to save.

Energetic: Challenge excites you.

Sense of Humor: Experts believe creativity can't occur without a touch of humor and I agree 100 percent. That's why I've tried to make this book at least thirty-five percent funny.

Self-actualizing: The desire to be all you can be. Affluent Artists™ are having so much fun. Their art and their finances have intersected to allow them to enjoy a happy, fulfilling life.

Self Discipline: It takes self discipline to finish a project all the way through. Conceiving the project is only part of the project.

Specific Interests: If you are really focused on your field, it might be almost impossible to focus on something like personal finance.

Severely Critical: You challenge almost everything. (Not a bad trait in evaluating investments either.)

Confident: The more creative you feel, the more confident you are. The less creative you feel, the more frustrated you are. (My suggestion is that creativity is enhanced when money is not a problem).

Risk-Taker: You really don't see what you are doing as a risk. You see it as a possible solution.

Persistent: Creative people do not give up on things easily. Once you can get around to creating your financial independence fantasy, nothing will deter you from making it a reality.

These characteristics of creative people are not ones that preclude someone from being good with money. In fact, you share many traits with fabulously successful investors. Some very creative people are very, very wealthy because of their art. So, yes you may be wired a little differently than the average person, but your enthusiasm, creativity, and willingness to take a risk give you the tools to be a better-than-average investor, too. You can always find someone to do the messy paperwork—you are very well equipped to handle your financial big picture.

I'M ABOVE IT ALL—I'M AN ARTIST!

Many artists feel a need to treat the real world with disdain, to be "anti" everything and, in my experience; this nihilism isn't a required trait for being a successful creative. Being different is not an inherently creative trait. It can imply that you are moving against something (or everything), or that you are in a state of rejection. Being against society or popular convention may be a desirable affectation for an artist but isn't necessarily one that will help you create. Some of the more successful artists I've talked with gain their creativity from being in a state of gratitude and grace, of peace and acceptance. The artist who has a low opinion of himself, society or even financial success may be limiting himself and his creativity with negative energy and pessimism.

Are there times when you can be a creative force by moving against the things that need to be acted against? Of course! Small, committed groups of people can change the world, but acting against *everything*, rejecting all of society, is probably not going to be productive. Creation comes from moving towards something, a positive step. It is difficult to imagine creation without a vision of hope. The Starving Artist persona is a negative one. Sure, you may have to pay your dues to get started—and there aren't many professions that don't make it hard on you at first—but rejecting the entire system is often a pre-made recipe for failure. Financial independence is part of the system we reject when we take that path.

Self-sabotage is known in every walk of life, in every human endeavor. The person who is rejecting society is actually providing himself with a roadmap to failure. Someone who is insecure about his art and worries that no one will buy it will reject society first. None of us would understand his work anyway. We are not up to his standards of excellence, he claims, so the Starving Artist rejects us first. It has been my experience that the person who has resigned himself to poverty by doing so is actually someone who doesn't want to make the sacrifice necessary to become successful as an artist, or in any other profession, or he fears the risks and challenges he'll face if he tries. Art is merely his cover. (I'm guessing that's not who is reading this book.)

NO TIME FOR MONEY, I'M TOO BUSY WORKING

The other side of the same coin is the artist who is so successful that he can't be bothered worrying about money. Work is so much fun, so fulfilling, so energizing that he doesn't want to come out in the real world and pay attention to mundane things like money. This strategy works as long as you have a lifetime contract to do whatever you want creatively, benefits that cover all of your needs, and the type of work that you will always want to do. (Let me know how that works out for you. Companies get bought out, managers retire and people get bored). Having financial independence is as important to you as it is to the street musician. In fact maybe more so, since you have more to lose!

I recently talked with a disabled veteran who had his dream job as an animator for a major studio taken away by a corporate cut. His dream was downsized. His next work was on a contract basis and included no benefits. He wished he had taken better notes when the human resource people tried to tell him about savings plans and other benefits that might be helping him now.

Our goal for you is financial independence—so your money is taking care of you because you took care of it. It's about paying enough attention to money to get in a systematic savings plan, to make some sacrifices now so that you'll have independence later. As far as I can tell, you are not hard-wired against this possibility. When it comes to money and finance, you are not that different from anyone else—at least not in this respect. We all avoid pain and seek pleasure. It's human nature.

Your interests may lie in things other than finance. I understand, believe it or not, mine do too! Reading the *Wall Street Journal* is a chore for me. I'd much rather be snorkeling in the Caribbean, but I've found that mastering a few fundamentals, exercising some discipline, and paying attention to my money gets me a lot more time on the beach!

Having an awareness of money and setting some money goals is a good idea for anyone, but it's especially important for someone who wants to live a creative, independent life. The path I'm encouraging you to take is one that eventually lets you have financial independence so you can be as creative as you want to be. You can have it all, but it requires a few skills and a little discipline. We've already established that successful creative people have what it takes to become successful money people.

WHAT I DID FOR LOVE

WHAT NO CUT CONTRACT?

CHAPTER 3: When it comes to the uncertainty of a career, artists are a lot like athletes: the stress and strain on a dancer's body is almost identical to an NBA player's. Torn-up knees, bad backs, stress fractures, and even the weight gain that comes with getting older are just some of the enemies of the dancer's career. Dancers, unlike professional athletes, don't have multimillion-dollar contracts, signing bonuses, or fat pension plans.

An actress can only play an ingénue for so long, composers may fall out of favor, and I know talented animators who have been replaced by computers. In fact, more than anyone who has a job in any industry, artists realize that their talents and their marketability may be fleeting. Having a good relationship with money, and having a sound financial plan, is even more important for someone who has chosen the creative life than someone trying to survive a career in corporate America.

I've seen *A Chorus Line* at least ten times. I know that artists do what they do for love. Or, they do it because they don't know what else to do, because their art won't let them do anything else, or because it's just so much fun. The multi-talented artist is the luckiest one, in this respect. The dancer who can choreograph, the singer who can write best-selling books, or the actor who learns to direct can channel their creative energy into their new profession. Chances are these people didn't just luck into their second careers. They were well-regarded by their colleagues. They planned and studied their new profession, and they had a fallback plan. But, as one of my friends said, "Having some money in the bank gives you more choices."

Having a good relationship with your money will give you a lot more options if your first career is about to end. The dancer who saved her money will be able to buy into a dance studio, an actor might produce a film, and the writer might tour the world researching his next project. One of the cornerstones of The Affluent Artist Method™ is the concept of building a nest-egg, making sacrifices for your art by doing what is needed to become financially independent, and by striving to reach the point where your money can take care of you because you have taken care of your money.

Remember M.C. Hammer? He was living the good life, wasn't he? One day, the bank came and took back his house. If you get the big financial break that you deserve, realize that your career could end up being a lot like that of many professional athletes: short-lived. Live below your means, put away some money for the long-term, some for the intermediate term, and go have some fun with the rest. If you buy that mansion for cash, realize you still have to pay property taxes, insurance, and utilities. If you buy Hummers for everyone in your family, remember you have to put gas in them too. Teaching yourself that money is a limited resource—once you spend it, it's gone—is not something all of us learn in childhood. But something you almost certainly did learn in childhood applies here: Better late than never!

YOU: THE IDEA FACTORY

If you were a cattle rancher... I know, this seems random; bear with me, I'm brainstorming here... You live in Texas now and you've begun raising cattle. Two of your cows (Well, you *thought* they were both cows!) had a calf. (A cub? Whatever!) Pretty soon, someone came along and offered you money for the calf and you figured out that you might be on to something. Before you knew it, you built a barn, bought more land, and sold more and more of your cattle. (Only as pets—your customers agreed they were not to be eaten.) Your free-range cattle became known throughout the land and that's how you became a cattle baron. You figured out, as the calves and customers kept coming, that you had to reinvest some of your calf money to do a few basic things like buy feed (cow food?) and build some fences to make sure the cattle didn't wander off. You could keep this going for as long as there was a market for baby cows (only as pets!).

As an artist, you have to take care of your ability to create in the same manner you took care of your cattle. You've got to be a cattle baron because you invested some of your income back into your business. In fact, you figured out how to be *in* the cow business. Practically speaking, investing money is your way of keeping the new creations coming, or making sure that you are sufficiently financially healthy to create more when the demand for your creation arises. Any business owner (cattle rancher, manufacturer, financial planner, etc.), figures out what to do to stay profitable and to continue on in business. Like a cattle baron, an artist is in the *creation business*. You have to figure out a business model that works for you. It's kind of fun to think of yourself as an idea factory, isn't it? It's very liberating to define yourself as a professional daydreamer—now you just have to pick a business model to make it work.

PSST, HERE'S THE PLAN...

In our office, the financial planning we do for an athlete or an artist includes a very different discussion than we might have with someone in a more typical corporate career. We focus on your hopes and dreams beyond your current job. What happens when this book is through its cycle? When the tour is over? When the exhibition ends? Is there a way that we can keep the income coming in when the paychecks stop? Making the Broadway touring company is a dream come true—is there a way to financially leverage that dream when the show closes?

A good parachute for an artist is to plan to set money aside to buy a business, pay tuition, or finance a new project. Often we want to accumulate assets that will throw off income and allow our artistic client's money to support him until he goes on to his next creative journey. The artist who has a creative block because money is in short supply is a grumpy artist and probably not a very productive one. Such artists end up writing technical manuals for septic systems, starring in celebrity reality shows, or selling their memorabilia on eBay.

We focus on having a long-term plan for some income streams, such as royalties, and extra per-diem money to get us through the leaner times between paying jobs. We often look at things like tax-free bonds, growth stocks, and dividend-paying investments to provide potential income and growth of principle. We also look at tax-sheltered investments such as personal retirement accounts. If we can defer income in your higher-earning years, you'll pay fewer taxes now and have a greater income stream later.

If our artist is self-employed, we have many options to defer current income and lower income taxes. Self-employed people can select business structures like Subchapter S corporations (those regulated by the provisions in subchapter S, Chapter 1, of the Internal Revenue Code) and they may be able to take advantage of a variety of pension plans, things with such names as SEP, Simple Profit Sharing, and Keogh. We can buy deferred investments from a variety of investment and insurance companies that are designed for the self-employed person. Being your own employer has many advantages and some disadvantages. Be sure that you talk with a financial planner and a tax consultant to make sure that you pay the taxes you have to pay and don't pay the ones that you can legally avoid.

ON THE ROAD AGAIN

Did I mention taxes? Let's not forget taxes! You have to file income taxes. Remember the public ordeal Willie Nelson endured with the IRS? He either ignored his accountants or had bad ones (depends on whose side of the story you believe) and didn't pay the kids at the IRS all the taxes that they thought they were entitled to. Willie ended up settling with the IRS for about $12 million, paying with the royalties from *The IRS Tapes: Who'll Buy My Memories?*, which he recorded just for them.

As a business person, you are responsible for paying taxes. If you go the self-employed route, you won't have an employer to withhold them for you. You'll have to send in your payments, usually quarterly, and have to pay something called a self employment tax. You'll also have to make your social security payments. We recommend you hire a bookkeeper or payroll service. We don't want you to end up singing for the IRS!

THE PATH LESS CHOSEN

Sometimes, the flip side of letting creative passion drive you is a disdain or disinterest in money. The artist who makes it, who actually finds a market for his art has a big decision to make. He can get a little education about personal finance or hire a good financial adviser and get comfortable with the idea of having money. The alternative is to overspend, live like there is no tomorrow, and forever be a Starving Artist.

You've met the Starving Artist: he'll always be broke, no matter how much money he might be holding. Even if he temporarily has a lot of cash, this guy is still starving. He has not come to peace with money. Someone who is uncomfortable with money will make sure they won't have it for very long. It's a validation of his insecurity. In my research, professional creative people treat their work like a business. They don't allow themselves to starve. They don't all become Wall Street whizzes, but they make sure they hire one!

The luckier starving artist will have a life partner or trusted business manager who handles the finances, pays the bills, balances the checkbook, and sets financial limits. As long as this person is around our starving artist is at least financially functional. Our artist is lucky enough to have a loved one or a hired gun to worry about mundane things like money. He can stay in the realm of creativity, somewhat sheltered from the real world as long as someone takes care of business for him.

Like some athletes, the more unfortunate starving artist may have a posse, a crew, or a collection of overly-dependent family members who have no idea how to handle large sums of money. (Actually they do have one idea: *You earn it, and we'll spend it!*) They only enable him to continue starving. If money only represents the material things you can have *now*, you will have a lot of material things. The artist who understands that money is a tool to build long-term security and future creativity is someone who is on her way to Affluence.

WHAT'S AN AFFLUENT ARTIST™?

The Affluent Artist™ is someone who understands that stewardship—the appreciation for and care of financial resources—is a signal back to the Universe that they can handle financial gifts. The Affluent Artist™ is someone who believes in abundance and understands that both his creativity and his financial resources are part of the Universe's abundance. Because of this understanding, he is confident that making good financial decisions will, in the long run, help him to make better creative decisions. Being free of anxiety or stress over money will allow his gift of creative energy to flow more freely and more often.

The Affluent Artist™ is not stingy or obsessed about money. She knows that the Universe is abundant and she can tap into its resources when she needs to. She is not afraid to take risks with money, to use her resources to further her art. The difference between the Affluent Artist™ and the Starving Artist is the comfort level she has with money and the knowledge of the wonderful things she can do with it. She knows that money can work for her, that there is no reason to avoid it. She knows that she deserves to be paid well for her creations and that by taking care of her money, she is demonstrating that she can take care of even more of it: the Universe can trust her with its abundance.

The Affluent Artists™ who know they have a short term gift, like my dancer daughters, know that they must prepare to find other creative outlets when their dancing days are over. When you show the Universe that you can handle its gifts, I believe the Universe will see that you receive more gifts. Your gift may next call you to teach, to design or to sponsor. It may call you to inspire your own dancer daughters. I hope you learn to be comfortable with the time you are paid for your gift and the time when you get to move on to your next one!

Affluence, then, is finding a confidence level with money. It's about knowing that you can use money as a tool to help you become more creatively fulfilled. Your business, your profession, requires that you take care of yourself, and that you put yourself in the best place to be creative at all times. Money is a tool to help you get there. The proper care and feeding of money will allow you to make the right creative career move. It will allow you to stay inspired because you know the agony and sweat you put in your art will be rewarded. It will allow you the pride of knowing that your gift has helped you care for your loved ones. We began by acknowledging that you do what you do for love, and there is no better reason to do anything than for love. We end this chapter by suggesting that love might just stick around a little longer if you can pay the bills!

MY WRITING SOUNDTRACK

When I think back on the time of my life I spent writing *The Affluent Artist*™, I'm sure that I'll remember Tomas Michaud's music as the soundtrack. If there is music in the waiting room to heaven, Tomas's New World Flamenco Jazz will be in the sound system. If it's possible to describe music as giving you a feeling of peace and stimulation at the same time, that would capture the essence of his work. I became such a fan that I called him and asked what he thought about this whole creation and money thing.

Tomas is a very humble guy, even though he has played with some very famous musicians and has a successful recording career of his own. He strikes you as somebody who is totally captivated by his art. Creativity is not something he claims to own. He likes to say he simply recorded his songs. He sees himself as an instrument of creation, not its source. He is humble. We had a very lively discussion about money, and I'd like to share some of it with you:

Affluent Artist ™ (AA): You have an interesting story about writing your song "Seville."

T.M.: I was on a trip to Spain and I was having this dream that I was listening to the stereo and I was really enjoying this song. So then I wake up and I'm lying in bed, and I still hear the melody and I'm laying there trying to think, "What CD is that on?" So it took me about 30 seconds to realize I hadn't recorded that song yet. So I grabbed my guitar and ran into the bathroom (I travel with a little recorder; I know I'm going to have ideas and I know better than to think I'll remember them) and I started playing what I heard. I thought I was being clever and didn't wake my partner, but she heard the whole thing!"

AA: I noticed you never claimed to write the song, you simply said you "recorded" it…

T.M.: That's my feeling about my music. It almost seems pretentious to say I created it. One way I think of it is that it comes to me, through me from the Universe. It could come from a variety of influences, some things I've heard as well as my experiences. The best things are things I don't try too hard about.

AA: How did you find this effortless creation?

T.M.: My earliest influences were sitting at the piano and going "Hey! That sounded good!" and getting the tape recorder out... It's most exciting when I wake up in the middle of the night. That's why I keep a recorder by the bed. I know better than to think I'll remember them. I've had to learn that experience, because if I don't, it's gone.

AA: Inspiration seems to come to you and you nurture it, but do you have a choice about it? Can you turn it off?

T.M.: I have a choice when I ignore it and roll back over and go to sleep! I've learned that I can't do that.

AA: Can you request it when you need it, like when you have a CD coming out?

T.M.: That's the million-dollar question, boy! I haven't figured out how to do that. I have tried, but there are some things that help, like if I make time to play my guitar every day. Traveling seems to help. That little change of being out of my environment helps me to be open to inspiration. It almost seems like if I try too hard, I block it. Going for walks on the beach seem to help... sometimes if I'm driving, something will come to me and I'll just hum it into my cell phone recorder.

A.A.: When you hear the song, do you hear the whole produced version, with a band?

T.M.: Usually just the melody and just a little portion of it. Then I'll sit with it for a little while and something else will come to me or I'll sit with it a little while and be doing something else and I'll go, "Oh that fits with that…"

A.A.: As you were growing up, at some point you had to make a decision to make your living as an artist, what was that like?

T.M.: Yea, I remember as a young person, being really torn with that because it was clear to me that my father wasn't okay with that. He grew up in the Depression and he really believed things like "money is hard to come by." It came out in a variety of ways, including when I was sitting there and playing my guitar and him yelling at me, "Go do something useful!"

A.A.: Nice!

T.M.: Or, "Go help me do something in the house," or, "Go do something to make money," and so for a long time there was this dichotomy of doing something I really loved to do and feeling irresponsible about it. Some of that, over the years, I've been able to sort out through introspection and meditation. One thing I did to sort of accommodate that is when I finished college I bought a music school. It's sort of my way to stay in music but to go into business, too. I've had to learn business skills and do something to make money.

A.A.: How's that been?

T.M.: Good, in some ways. It's helped me to learn some business skills and it has also been a distraction. In some ways I think I may have dragged it on too long. It's an on-going dilemma. I have a pretty good balance right now, where I have the business and it kind of runs itself. I spend about 25 hours a week on it.

A.A.: When you have business things on your mind, how does it affect creativity?

T.M.: It does seem to distract me when there are some problems and I don't know how I'm going to solve them. Fortunately, I have developed my business to the point where that doesn't happen very often.

A.A.: You have this creativity and you play your own music at this point in your career. But, having all of this creativity . . . what's it like to do something musically just for the money?

T.M.: Well, it's been fifteen years, but, at the time, it seemed okay. It's sort of like when you're an apprentice in the business, you are grateful that you have the opportunity to work with masters to learn the skills, but when you have the skills then it's not time to be an apprentice anymore. At that time it felt right, to be able to play with musicians who were better than me, to be able to imitate songs that were created by incredible songwriters and marvel at their chord changes and combination of melodies. And now I don't feel true to myself if I do that; even if I hear something really good, it's not mine.

A.A.: Do you have to make commercial sacrifices for that?

T.M.: I think that's one of the things that my business venture has helped with; it's provided me with an income so I don't have to make songs specifically for commercial or financial gain. But, there is always a sense of "how big an audience am I creating this for?"

A.A.: So you do keep the audience in mind…

T.M.: Not necessarily when I'm inspired and putting down an idea. But when I actually make a CD I pick songs based on who's going to be listening to this, how many CDs will I sell, or, is this song better for my own enjoyment and should I record it in some low-cost way?

A.A.: Have you ever found that money was a block?

T.M. (pause) I never really thought of it that way.

A.A.: Well, let's not put anything like that in there!

T.M.: I experience it more as a motivator. What kind of a cool idea can I come up with that will inspire me to make money and because of it, I can keep creating? The bottom line is, it will actually tap into my deep creativity. It's that "flow" experience.

A.A.: What's your career path, where would you like to go with it?

T.M.: I'd like to play for bigger audiences and I'd like my CDs to reach more people. I'm planning to spend the next five years writing and recording my music and then performing as a way of reaching out to people.

A.A.: How is your relationship with money, by the way?

T.M.: It's… ongoing. (laughs)

A.A.: Are you friends, are you speaking?

T.M.: Yea, actually, when you say that, I've really come a long way.

When I think about it, I come from a real poverty mentality, with my Father having lived through the Depression. I always heard how hard money was to come by and how you really had to be careful with it. And I really didn't realize how much that affected me. I've come a long way in the last five years of letting go of my Father's voice inside of me while still acknowledging it's there. I'm more okay with stepping into unknown territory… I've had the good fortune to receive sums of money from places where I could not go out and make it happen, a major corporation, about four years ago, gave me $45,000 to use my music! It turns out one of their VPs was a fan of mine. He'd been coming to my concerts and then, two years later they said, "Let's do it again!"

A.A.: No kidding!

T.M.: I could not make that happen, so it really gave me some concrete proof that I don't have to see where the money is coming from.

A.A.: So that answers my question about the Law of Attraction—you've already experienced it!

T.M.: Yes, and I'm sure there are many more things that await me, and not just financially. I've been able to find other musicians in my community who are on a spiritual path also.

A.A.: How so?

T.M.: It recently came to me to donate the profits from the sales of one of my CDs to help save the rainforests, and I'm also very concerned about animal rights.

A.A.: May I ask, without going into detail, how do you take care of your money?

T.M.: I realize the value of having a good financial planner, a good accountant, and a good attorney—people who can do things that I don't do that well.

A.A.: In doing my research, I've found that artists are all over the place when it comes to money. Some have a real block when it comes to money, but it seems like the ones who can resolve these issues are the ones who really prosper artistically and financially.

T.M.: It is something we need to resolve and I feel like I have room to grow there. I need to be more organized about how I take care of my money and invest it. I kind of find myself not wanting to look at it. I mean, I haven't looked at my financial statements in a month. Now there's something there, somebody who owns a business should be looking at his financial statements at least once a week, at least glancing at them! In investing, I feel a little baffled about what I'm supposed to be doing and when I'm supposed to be doing it, so there's some learning to be done there.

A.A.: You know, you've spent your life dedicated to your music. You can't be expected to approach finances with the same expertise!

T.M.: I appreciate that. It's just like my business: I have to be a man of many hats.

A.A.: Thomas, thank you so much for your time, your insights and especially your music!

INVESTING IS BORING!

"It's the lions and tigers that scare me."

CHAPTER 4: We are close enough now that I can make a confession to you: After 40 years of investing and 25 years as a professional investment adviser, I can finally admit that most Wall Street stuff bores me to death! I promise, the volumes of research reports, charts and graphs that most people think I've memorized don't even make it to my desktop. Go to a seminar and hear some stock analyst drone on about why their buy rating was the correct call (even though the stock dropped 50 percent after they recommended it)? No thanks, I'd rather not. Wall Street is an invigorating place—for some people. But you don't have to know all of that stuff to be a good investor. In fact sometimes I am convinced that you see things in a better light if you don't know all of the stuff that we professionals think we need to know.

MY TOOLBOX

My tools are financial instruments, rather than paintbrushes, chisels, or musical instruments, but like any instruments they are better used when they are asked to do the job they were designed to perform. I don't get too excited about the tools. I get very excited about goals. Investing money can help you do amazing things. I've seen it happen! I've seen people retire with grace, dignity and even a little mischief! I've helped kids go to medical school and seen vacation homes purchased because of what investing can do. What do you want to accomplish? If you begin to focus on your dreams, you'll be able to handle just enough of this money stuff to get by. Because, in reality, you can "rent" the expertise that you need. You can be a very successful investor by hiring a professional to help.

RELEASE YOUR GUILT

If you bought this book in spite of yourself, if you turn the radio station every time the stock market report comes on, if you feel guilty that you don't know what the business section of the paper even looks like, let that go. Stop beating yourself up. You really don't have to know everything about investing to get excited about investing. It's possible, for example, to play a song on the piano without knowing every piano piece ever written! You don't have to have a Masters in Finance to reach your money goals.

While I am confessing, let me tell you about the book *The Artist's Way*, by Julia Cameron. It's a course that anyone can follow to get past roadblocks. She teaches us how to give ourselves permission to be successful in our creative pursuits. She even talks about getting over your reluctance to deal with money! Financial discipline isn't this particular child's favorite thing, and financial acumen might have been the gift you traded off to become an artist. So if you can't make investing appealing to you, you need to make it fun. The fun comes from the expectation and hope of achieving bigger and greater goals—the kind of things that need money.

If you knew, for example, that adding to your 401(k) might help you open your own studio one day, you'd probably do it. If you want to be able to write that great travel guide to India, you'll need to have a financial plan that will allow you to get there. Setting concrete monetary goals and working the plan to achieve them is something that your inner artist can learn to tolerate, like, or maybe even get excited about. Just as children always behave when you promise them a treat, you can make your goal an especially vivid and desirable one if it means you're more likely to stick with your plan!

INVEST IN THINGS YOU LOVE

One of the first things I help my clients to do is find something to invest in that is meaningful. For the person who likes to travel, we might look at the cruise industry. For the person who enjoys running, we'll identify several sneaker companies. For the person who wants to help clean up the earth, we'll look for alternative fuel companies. There really is no limit to the type of investing that you can do so it's easy to find an investment that is aligned with your passions.

Many creative people are attuned to something called "socially conscious investing" or as I like to call it, "Putting your money where your heart is." Socially conscious investors avoid investing in industries they find objectionable, companies that follow environmentally unsound practices, trade with oppressive governments, or are not consumer friendly. Part of their investment logic is common sense: why invest in companies which might become the objects of class action lawsuits? But part of it is a question of karma. If you want to make the world a better place, your portfolio is an excellent place to start! If you are inclined to invest in this manner, you will need a good money manager whose investment principles will match yours. Check my website for links to some of them (www.AffluentArtist.com).

REPETITION, REPETITION

Have you ever read the instructions on a bottle of shampoo? "Wash, rinse, repeat." That's why my daughters take such long showers: they keep washing their hair over and over! Getting in the habit of saving and investing is more about the when than it is about the where. Most people, whether creative are not, only save when they can't touch the money, like in a 401(k). Baby boomers are infamous for having all of their money locked up in their retirement plan or their home equity. Why? Because they have to make their mortgage payments and they never see the money that goes into their company retirement plan. Otherwise, I have learned, they would never save a dime.

We'll talk more when we get to artistic paths and the various ways that you can put money away before you see it, but the important thing is that you figure out a way to hide money from *yourself*. As I said, I have met people from very ordinary jobs, with low pay, who have amassed fortunes because they systematically saved money. Finding something to invest in is not as important as actually doing the investing. A program of systematically putting money away is the foundation for financial independence. You don't have to be a Wall Street genius to have money taken out of your paycheck every month, but you have to be disciplined enough to do it and strong enough to leave it alone.

A LITTLE THERAPY

So let's get real for a minute: what is the problem with investing, anyway? I think it comes down to self-doubt, or even fear. As a creative person, your career lives and dies by the sword of rejection: you can be sent home from auditions because you're not the right type, your screenplay might be shelved, your great idea might be shut down by a committee. Or the sword may strike someone else so you can live to create another day. Either way, you're not in a hurry to create more self-doubt by making the wrong investments and losing money. You may simply spend whatever you make in celebration of your creative survival!

I know creative people who feel inadequate about the way they handle money because someone told them, "You have no head for business." (You really don't need to grow *another* head for business, no more than I have an actual second left foot for dancing.) Maybe that someone was their parents or some rich friends (with inherited money.) Someone gave them the investment-advice equivalent of "Girls aren't good at math" and they bought it. They have great self-esteem when it comes to their inner artist, but their inner investor needs a hug! Your creative success requires the highest quality canvases, a superbly crafted guitar, or a precision photographic instrument. Don't let your financial success depend on someone who won't—or can't—give you her best.

WHO COULD BENEFIT FROM YOUR WEALTH?

I've asked this question of you before and I'm going to ask it again: "How creative could you be if money wasn't an issue?" The question that goes with that is, "How many people could you help if you had the resources to do so?" When you don't have any money, you are limited to donating your time and effort. But if you want to do great things for many people, you need to build wealth! Wealth for its own sake isn't something most creative people value, but having the wealth to be financially independent and using some of it to help people is something to be proud of.

Let me share one of my personal goals with you. I have this vision that one day I'll meet the president and treasurer of a Little League in an impoverished community and I will ask them this question, "How many more children would play baseball or softball in your league if you didn't have to charge them an annual fee?" I want to be able to write a check so as many children as possible have an opportunity to play baseball in that neighborhood. And I want to buy those kids all of the equipment, even their sneakers. I don't want to buy them baseball shoes. I want to buy them sneakers because they can't wear baseball shoes to school. This vision is so real I can feel the dirt under my feet as I stand on the baseball field and write the check. I can feel the checkbook in my hand and I can feel the pen between my fingers as I sign my name. I can feel the tear of gratitude on my cheek for having been given the resources to accomplish this wonderful goal. I know that it will take a lot of money to achieve this goal, so I am very excited and guilt-free about wanting to accumulate the wealth that it will take. I have a vision of writing that check— I see it every day.

I'm sure your thing isn't youth baseball. Your goal might be saving the rain forests, helping young writers, or digging wells in African villages. Everyone I know has someone that they would love to help. But having a goal that will allow you to make a real difference in the world is a motivational tool that will help you to feel a whole lot better about money and wealth. You can start with a modest goal—buy one family Thanksgiving dinner—and get bigger goals as you accumulate more money. You are only limited by your dreams.

IT'S NOT *THAT* COMPLICATED

You can invest with a minimal knowledge of financial markets. You don't have to be a day-trader; you don't have to have your broker's office on autodial. Warren Buffett, the most successful investor in history, doesn't even have a computer in his company office. What you need is an overview of where financial markets are going. You need to know roughly where to invest money and then you just need to, as they tell the voters in Chicago, invest early and invest often!

Having an overview of the financial markets is very important and I'd like to give you a sample investment outlook. I get a general, long-term view of the world in place before I make an investment, and I try not to overhaul it too often. World events will affect the short-term performance of the market, but I'm not trading, I'm investing for the long-term. I keep up with global trends and new technologies, identify places where growth might create tremendous demand, and then determine which countries, industries, and companies will benefit most as a result. Then, well, I'm getting more complicated than I need to, here's how it might work in real life... (Fade to Wall Street, young guy, his tie loose, on the phone and calm amidst the chaos of the trading floor . . .)

"Joe, you know when you call India to get your computer fixed? I just read this book by Thomas Friedman, *The Earth is Flat,* and he says the guy who answers that phone probably holds a master's degree and was one of maybe 5,000 people to apply for the privilege of answering the phone when you called. This job that's been outsourced to him from the U.S. is his ticket out of poverty. It'll bring his family and future generations into a middle class lifestyle that they couldn't have imagined just a few years ago. That guy is the new consumer. I think he's the backbone of the world economy. He'll need everything: a refrigerator, food to put in it, a car, a car loan, gasoline to put in the car, tires, cement for his driveway, clothes, a mortgage, insurance. You get the idea! India, the largest democracy in the world, is about to become the American consumer on steroids.

"Think about that guy in India, then multiply him by that country's population and then add in an even bigger emerging middle class in China, the rest of Asia, Eastern Europe, Russia, and South America. You have a pretty strong case to be made for investing in the global economy. If the twentieth century was the American century, I believe the 21st century will be the global century. Capitalism has won, communism lost, and thanks to technology and communications the entire world wants to be the American consumer.

"Joe, we should position ourselves in the industries and companies that are poised to take advantage of global growth—companies that will provide the basic infrastructure and consumer goods that will be in demand in growing societies." (Our hero helps his client get invested in a diversified portfolio that will be poised to profit from global growth. He won't call his client in six weeks with a whole new story either. Their outlook is a long term view that will stay in place a very long time. Fade out . . .) *

Long-term investors, and I am one, actually have it pretty easy. I didn't have to interview any CFOs, consult any charts, or throw any darts to identify global trends. I just had to be paying attention. I let professional money managers identify the best growth and value opportunities for me. I don't have to watch that guy on CNBC run around and scream and shout every time a stock goes up five cents, and I don't have to reinvent the wheel every time I want to put a little money away. Once I am comfortable with my global overview, I simply look to find investments to match it. Yes, it's possible to have more than one investment theme, (healthcare, energy, technology, etc.) In fact, it's a good idea. But start with one.

THE BUMPER STICKER METHOD

Remember, I've been investing professionally for a quarter of a century and I'm telling you that *I* don't like to make complicated decisions. I like to keep it simple and you can do the same thing. You don't have to know *everything* about *everything* to invest. You need to know something about something! Once you've clearly formulated a worldview as it pertains to investing, pass on any investment opportunity that doesn't align with it. I'm not going to invest in an Internet dog food company if I think global water delivery is my theme. I emphasize that it's a sound idea to let a professional select the specific stocks, bonds, or other investment vehicles once you've identified a theme. They just know more than we do.

* Note from the Kids in Compliance: International investing involves special risks, including currency fluctuations, differing financial accounting standards and possible economic and political volatility. Sector investments are companies related to business in a certain sector. They may be subject to fierce competition and their products and services may be subject to rapid obsolescence. They are additional risks associated with investing in individual sectors, including limited diversification.

When making an investment decision or describing a recommendation to a client; I ask myself if I could describe it on a bumper sticker. You know, a quick phrase, one that would explain the essence of your investment if you saw it stuck to the bumper of a Chrysler? If I can't, I probably don't want to bother. Sure there's more to investing than finding a catchy phrase but I only have so much money to invest. I'm not going to put any of it in places that I can't comprehend. I can sleep with missing the next great investment opportunity, but I can't sleep if I'm worried about investing my money in something that I don't comprehend.

Don't become paralyzed into inaction because you're bored by financial stuff. Do you know how much money you'll have in ten years if you don't save any? That's right, not enough! Why not imagine your abundance, get over your blocks and fears about money. Challenge your inner artist to come over and play in the money sandbox. You might find out that she likes it there!

THE BUSINESSMAN AS ARTIST

Laverne Gehman is a talented and well-regarded interior designer in Harrisburg, Pennsylvania, and he almost lost his inner artist because of the pressures of running a business. He has been at the helm of his firm, Classic Interiors, for over twenty years and has built a thriving family business. We've talked a lot about artists being uncomfortable with business, but Laverne is a case study in the opposite. The pressures and challenges of running a successful design firm, managing inventory and employees, overseeing installations, and dealing with finance was taking him away from his true talent: meeting with clients and creating fantastic designs. I talked with him about creativity and money by phone from my Florida office:

A.A.: So Laverne, do you consider yourself an artist?

L.G.: Oh absolutely. I started in the business. Well, I didn't set out to start a business. My father had a furniture store and passed away very early. I had grown up in the business and felt an obligation to help my mother. Later, I reached a point where it was time to stop working for my mom and open my own business. It was a big decision to leave the family business and go out on my own, you have no idea. I had to move away so I didn't compete with my mom or even appear to compete with my mom. I didn't put my name on the business, so I could be anonymous in that respect. I had a wife and kids at home and I did everything I could to build the business. I did everything from the design work to installing the draperies. I started with a real passion, but I kind of lost that after a while.

A.A.: Tell me about that.

L.G.: I only just regained the passion for the creative side of the business. I've gone from a one-man shop to a 30,000 square foot showroom with warehouse accommodations and 14 employees. So I've been really saddled with running a business. Some of the passion and joy from doing the creative stuff kind of got lost. I went through a process recently where I couldn't find my passion. I didn't know about the direction I wanted to go in, and I was thinking about selling my business. The process helped me to realize that I still have my passion to create and for the creative side of the business. I realized that all the business stuff was just things that had to be dealt with. I've already made some personnel changes to allow me to do what I love.

A.A.: So, I'm hearing you say that business and money have kind of blocked your creativity?

L.G.: Yes, somewhat, the need to keep this whole business going. And you know, this whole Law of Attraction thing, I have this CD I keep in my car and it talks about not focusing on things like, "I need the money, I need the money" and to focus on true joy and happiness. It seems to be working. I've been writing tons of new business even though my core market, newly built homes, is going through a rough time. So the new business I've been finding comes back to our core strength, which is design work. I'm really excited because that's the kind of work I love to do.

A.A.: So you are just focusing on doing work that makes you feel more fulfilled?

L.G.: Yes, I'm promoting somebody to operations manager and making other changes to keep me doing the creative work. I stopped resisting any outcome. For a while I had a real fear that I was going to go out of business. There was a real terror attached to that. I just started to be thankful and look at my blessings, to be real thankful for the things I have. You know what, if my business goes one way or the other, I'm going to observe it. I'm not going to be panic-stricken. It's not who I am. I'm going to take action, of course.

A.A.: It's clear you are going to get through that—you aren't going to fail. Could I get back to the creative part for a minute? Did you go to school for interior design?

L.G.: No, I did not. They say the apple doesn't fall far from the tree.

I was always artistic— artistic things come easily to me. I've always had an eye for color and space. I can picture things. I grew up on a farm and my Dad always wanted a church. He bought an old church, renovated it, and went into business. Basically, because my Mom was a freelance interior designer, our own home was always beautiful. Even though she never graduated high school, she was an amazingly talented interior designer. People would see her home and say, "Would you come and design our home?" I was just in high school when they opened it. I was planning to become a chiropractor. In fact I went to Palmer College to study. But, in my first semester, my parents were in a real bind and I felt obliged to help them. So I left school to join the firm. I was there for like 15 years before I came here. So my creativity, a lot of it, comes from my Mom and training under her. People come to me all the time and say, "Do I need to go to school to become an interior designer?" I'll have four-year-degree interior design people come to me and they have no innate ability. The design schools don't really give them a lot of good tools to work with.

A.A.: What's it like for you? I mean, do you just walk in a room and see the way it should look?

L.G.: Yeah, sometimes I walk in a room and I can't stop laughing. The cool thing is I've seen this room. I mean, my people have done all the installations and I do a final walk-through. I've seen this room in my mind. The visualization is paramount. There are people doing interior design who really can't do this. They don't have that innate tool. If you've got the gift, you've got it. If you don't, you don't have it. There are tools you can use to enhance it. For example, our business is a lot of new construction. Yesterday, people brought me a blueprint. I wrote orders for new floor covering and I had to be able to visualize from the two-dimensional to the finished product. For us, it's a matter of putting all the colors and materials together along with traffic patterns, furniture layout and everything else.

A.A.: I talked with a composer who talks about songs just coming to him while he is sleeping or walking on the beach.

L.G.: People ask me, "How do you come up with these ideas?" And a lot of people in my business take credit for everything they do, as if it is 100 percent original, but we are all more or less editors. There is nothing I do that hasn't already been done. You talk about things coming to artists from the Universe. Well, to me, I see a hotel lobby, I see magazines, I see photographs, and it's all those inputs that I've seen that create my point of view when I talk about myself as more or less an editor. I edit the ideas I've seen. I might take elements from five different designs I've seen and put them together in one room. Now that's my interpretation. That's what makes what I do unique. We do get a bit of a signature on the things I do. But I do pride myself on listening to the customer and designing a room according to the customer's taste, not necessarily my taste. I spend time with my clients and ask a lot of questions about how they live, kids, pets etc. Then I use my talents to find something that they will like. I love it when they look at my first presentation and say, "That's it! We would have never gotten this if we hadn't met you?" I use the term innate because it isn't something that I do consciously. It's just the way I see things.

A.A.: Do you have other artistic outlets?

L.G.: Well, let's see. I have taken accordion lessons, but I've stopped because of my schedule. But no, do I paint or do anything like that? No.

A.A.: Is money a motivation to you?

L.G.: I have designers who come to me and say, "I am not in sales. I just want you to know that I am a designer, not a sales person." Well, I just look at them and smile. I wonder why they are even interviewing with me for a job. I mean, first and foremost you have to sell me on you. People think somehow they have to be creative without having any attachments and not do the fiscal side of it. Unless you inherited wealth and just do this as a recreation, that's one thing. But, in my world, I've always had to be productive.

A.A.: I think that's kind of the premise of the book.

L.G.: It doesn't do you a lot of good in this life, I mean the artists who only get appreciated after they are dead. Somebody else is reaping millions for work that they did. In other words, if I'm in the right place, work is not drudgery to me. If I'm truly where I'm supposed to be, my work is only an outcome of where my joy is. I'm doing this because this is what I do. I love my life, and it's a passion. I feel so much closer to that than I did just a few months ago.

A.A.: What would you do if you won the lottery or somehow gained financial independence?

L.G.: I'd become very selective in the jobs I take, and I'd say no more often. I would continue to do what I do. I would be totally true to myself and only do what I really want to do. If you'd asked me this question a few months ago, I might not have answered the same way. I was really unhappy.

A.A.: How are you with money?

L.G.: I witness, first hand, some people who seem to not enjoy spending their money. I've always been the opposite of that. When I go buy a car, I truly enjoy it because I feel like I've earned it. I mean, what do I work so hard for? I feel like I've earned it. It's come to me, I'm blessed with it. I never beat people up for the price. If you want to talk about it from a Christian standpoint, if you want to talk about it from the Law of Attraction, I believe that's what I want to put out there in the Universe. I want service. I want to be taken care of, but I'm a full price kind of guy.

A.A.: Okay, so you are good at spending money. How about investing it?

L.G.: Well, a guy like you will have a heyday with me! Up until about three or four years ago, every penny I had went back into the business. I had kids to put through college too. We always own the real estate for our building. I don't have a lease or pay rent, so I've invested in real estate. We set up a plan for my employees. We match funds and I do it for myself too. We invest regularly. It's been kind of a slow deal for me, but I believe I could sell the business at some point. But, it will be hard to know what the investment is worth, especially being a mom-and-pop. I'm trying to put some systems in place to make sure the business can function without me. A lot of my business is the creativity that is attached to me, but probably half of my business is being written by people other than me.

A.A.: Thanks, I truly appreciate your time. Thanks for being open with us.

WHEN MONEY BLOCKS YOU

"Next case: the Internet economy versus
millions of investors who should have known better."

CHAPTER 5: This book is largely about helping creative people get *past their block about money*, but in doing my research, I decided that it was important that we talk a little about what happens *when money blocks you*. I was really tempted to stop right here, to demonstrate writer's block and say, "I got nothing" and leave the next five pages completely blank, but common sense and my editor prevailed.

I know it happens. There are times when you can't get in your creative space because money is such an issue or because the idea of having to adjust your creativity to a customer's demands takes all the joy and passion away. In the interviews I've conducted, I've found that artists are often called to create by a force beyond their control and it's a call they can't decline. Following your calling puts you on a different career path than your friends with MBAs, dental practices, or engineering careers.

Sometimes you wonder if it's all worth it, if you will ever make a decent living at this art thing. After all, your parents told you to get a real job! Money can and does get in the way of creativity. Creating becomes difficult because we are angry with our situation and we wonder if we've made the right choices. Money isn't the only reason we block, of course, but it's a common one. I'd like to tell you about some things that have worked for me and for some of my friends. I'm a financial guy who knows artists, not a shrink, so consider this the opinion of a friend.

COULD YOU JUST LET IT GO, JUST FOR A MINUTE?

I have the joy of having met a wonderful spirit called Hale Dwoskin. He's the author of *The Sedona Method* and one of the teachers featured in *The Secret*. Hale claims to live in Sedona, Arizona, but I think he really lives in the North Pole and makes toys. Hale has a calmness and joy about him that seems to infuse any space he enters. My experience is that his method of dealing with stress and anxiety is a blessing to anyone who tries it. I recommend that you read his book, listen to one of his tapes, or attend one of his seminars.

The essence of the Sedona Method is this: you can control your emotions, your thoughts, and your impulses. Hale teaches you to release your anxieties. His method helps you to feel an inner calmness, and its simplicity is surprising. People have been known to drop life-long phobias after a short introduction to the Sedona Method. My personal experience is that the Sedona Method is a very useful tool to allow you to stay fully present, avoid distraction, and get in that Flow we are all seeking. When you are able to recognize your anxieties about things like money and then release them, you are left in a space that allows you to feel more at peace and more able to plug into your true essence and creativity. I like to think of myself as living "in grace" when I am releasing as Hale has taught me. I feel as though I have a greater capacity to understand what is swirling around in my busy mind and can choose which thoughts I need to act on and which ones I can release. One of the best things about the Sedona Method is that it is so simple and easy to learn. I'd recommend that you give it a try.

COME OUT AND PLAY

One successful artist I interviewed said this about money and motivation, "I just try to think of what cool thing I can come up with that people will want." He recognized that money is a tool that can help him create, once he stopped fighting it. Another artist I know teaches music to pay the bills. The inspiration he gets from his students helps him create music that he knows someone will buy.

Sometimes it is a good idea to return to the very basic, most simple elements of any problem. If your child was having trouble with something, what would you do to help? With children, you make things as basic and simple as you can, and then add love. Julia Cameron, author of *The Artist's Way*, tells us our inner artist is our playful self, your inner child. It doesn't function well when the adults are worried about things like rent, child support, or car payments. Remove the money worries, and do something fun to help yourself reconnect with the joy and excitement that comes from creation. You can do it. It's okay if it feels silly, that's a good thing! Maybe that burst of joy is all you need to help rekindle your passion!

CAN YOU RELEASE YOUR LIMITS?

In the corporate world, frustration can really set in. You can feel like your integrity is compromised for the sake of business and money only so often before you don't want to play anymore. The perception that your art is not art that can be produced for profit might come from fear. If you believe that you only have a limited amount of creativity that you can draw from the Universe, you can't imagine using it up for mere currency. The person who lets money block her is afraid that there isn't enough money in the Universe and hasn't tapped into the concept that you can have all of the money that you need. The universe is waiting for you to align yourself and it will deliver.

Once you accept that feeling (and even welcome your block) you will stop fighting it and something magical begins to happen: you relax. Now that you have accepted that feeling, Hale would ask you to imagine being able to release it, to let it go. If you could, when would you let go of it? How about now? When you see Hale do this in person, it's amazing. People physically change, tension visibly disappears.

I think you can get past a money block, I really do. Money is something that can be used to accomplish wonderful things. For example, if you wanted to help one young person learn how to paint, you could do it by yourself, but you only have so much time. A wealthy, successful artist can sponsor a student or even an entire school. Hundreds of kids could learn how to paint because of your art! Your block about money might seem like it is about not having enough or about money corrupting your art, but money is just something that you are viewing in a restrictive manner. It is your view of money that needs to change and that's something that you can do!

Artists have a unique position in life. They really don't have capacity constraints. A factory can only build so many widgets. Once it's working three shifts and using all of its productive resources, it can't produce anymore. As a creative person you are channeling your work from the limitless Universe. You can always produce when you really need to. Increase your limits—they are self-imposed anyway. Better yet, eliminate them altogether! The fact that money can motivate some people and completely paralyze others proves that it *isn't the money*, it's the individual. Let me say this with love: grab a mitt and get in the game. We need you!

THE HOLLYWOOD PSYCHIC

Joanna Garzilli is an A-list star. Her Hollywood clients will not do a deal or sign a contract without talking to her first. They won't tempt fate! Joanna is not only a creative person in her own right; she is also someone who spends a lot of time talking with creative people. Joanna has appeared on television and radio and is also an author and life coach. She believes that we all have the ability to unleash our psychic powers, and her workshops are designed to help people do just that. She has lived the Starving Artist and the Affluent Artist lifestyles. I think her insights are worth passing on to you (Yes, she was expecting my call!):

A.A.: Do you make a living as a psychic?

J.G.: Absolutely.

A.A.: Tell me about that, how does your business work? How do you charge, for example?

J.G.: Well, I've built my business over the years and I charge by the hour, usually in half-hour blocks. If it is someone who has come to me before and just has a question, I do fifteen minutes. If it is someone who is new, they have a lot of questions, so I recommend a half an hour. I've shifted my practice in the last few years. I used to meet with everyone in person, now I do more consultations over the phone. When I was doing my TV show, I just didn't have time to see people in person.

A.A.: What kind of things do people want to know?

J.G.: They want to know everything, and focus on the main things in life: love, relationships, career, family, finances, health, friendships and ultimately, which is slightly separate from career, "what is my life purpose?" Those are the important questions. Some people are afraid they are being selfish or narcissistic in asking such questions, but I really believe that a psychic helps you to see where you are in your unconscious mind and where you will be in your future. So, if you make sure you want to do things right, you see a psychic to ground that information and apply it to your life. So I think it is very wise to ask those things.

A.A.: So it's like a spiritual coaching.

J.G.: Exactly. But it is grounded. Some of my clients have been bankers, surgeons, housewives, and insurance brokers. Oddly enough, in the last few months, I've had more people from financial institutions asking and I've had movie producers ask about how to structure a financial deal, so it becomes a combination of looking into my knowledge in working in some of those areas and then being able to tap in psychically beyond that. I can see the big picture and suggest they don't go with the deal for a while or set it up differently. I'll give one example: a client of mine was going to Australia to do a movie and I suggested, very strongly, that the finances for the movie weren't going to come together. She needed to line up other work in television, and the movie financing would come together at a later date. She phoned me up several months later (she was so optimistic this was going to work) and told me that it happened exactly the way I said. It did come together at a later date. So, when you are about to give more challenging information, you want to present it as a positive and give information that can turn a negative into a positive.

A.A.: Your website describes your first encounter with a spirit guide. How much of what you see is coming from a psychic place and how much is just your own wisdom? And, can you tell the difference?

J.G.: Yea, I can absolutely tell the difference. I've had different spirit guides. It's kind of like going to school. You progress from elementary school, to middle school, to high school and then college, and you get different teachers along the way. I've met different guides. I draw from what I like to call my Higher Self. Each person, all of us, have the ability to tap into that. It's like radio waves. We don't see them but we know they exist. It's that way with psychic energy. I feel like I can hear and see energy without an x-ray machine. Psychic again is just a label, a way to define me and put me in a box.

A.A.: I'm glad you said that. I was just going to ask a question. I've talked to everyone from musicians to authors, and they all say their creativity comes from someplace they can't define. You are calling it psychic energy but I think you are describing the same thing.

J.G.: Absolutely, the word psychic is just from another angle. I just think it's human nature to want to categorize things and put them in boxes. A lot of the time we are fearful about what we don't know. When someone works intuitively, that's abstract, so the label helps people to understand it. One of the things I've warned people about are the neon sign psychics—they don't have any authenticity about them. They are exploiting people for money. I don't want to be compared to them.

A.A.: In every industry there are bad guys. You seemed to get past that.

J.G.: I realized if you are really good at something, it's okay to charge for it. A lot of people say psychics shouldn't charge for readings, that it's a spiritual thing and it's gift. Well, being a great actor is a gift, being able to do surgery is a great gift, being able to work with finances and design great portfolios is a gift. So why can't people who have an intuitive ability charge for it?

A.A.: Well, that's pretty much what my book is about: about artistic people feeling comfortable getting paid for their art. Did you have to reconcile that?

J.G.: Absolutely. I went from growing up in an affluent family, having gone to the best private schools, getting a higher education, having five-star vacations and hanging out with a lot of very wealthy people. I was fine until I started using my intuitive ability. I was in that sort of new age world. I got a lot of criticism from people around me saying, "Well, it's not spiritual to have money." I just felt embarrassed, coming from a family with money, owning my home and having everything I needed. I basically threw the baby out with the bathwater, because somebody I was dating held that belief very strongly. I was in love and basically naïve at that point. I basically gave away all my money because I felt guilty for having it. I lost everything—my home, everything—and I actually went into pretty heavy debt. It was really challenging for me because I thought: well, I'm going to be rescued by my connections to my spirit guide and God. I perceive God as pure energy. I believe all the different religions, it's all the same thing for me.

So I suddenly realized that I wasn't going to be rescued—that I had to deal with all this stuff—so I got myself out of that relationship and started back at square one. I realized if I hadn't felt guilty about using my spiritual gift to make a living that I could have been a millionaire. So, my home now is worth well over a million dollars and all the things I have, I learned the hard way. So, when people say "you shouldn't charge for what you do," they can go jump.

I talk about it in my workshops. There are times to charge and times not to charge. There was a situation when I was working at MTV. I was a producer then and I was talking to someone on the phone who I called to be on a TV show. I asked to speak with her daughter. She said she was so sorry, but she had passed over several months ago. I ended up picking up on her daughter. I first asked her Mom how she was doing. She said she was so devastated and just wished she could know her daughter was all right. At that point, her daughter came through to me and I passed on a message to her Mom. It was pretty wild.

A.A.: How did the Mom take that?

J.G.: She was very grateful. Just five hours earlier she was in complete despair and couldn't understand why this happened. She just wanted some peace of mind, some kind of confirmation. Some of the specific things I gave her were some things her daughter would have said. The fact that she would have been on that show was a real comfort to her as well. She knew how much her daughter wanted to be on that TV show.

A.A.: Did you worry, even for a second, that she could have gone the other way and slammed down the phone and call your boss?

J.G.: No, I was very casual. I didn't just say, "I'm a psychic." I started with counseling and then from there went into a little more. You never want to push information on someone. Another time I was in a café in London and someone was in a funk, in a bad place, and his Father came through. I didn't say, "Oh, your Dad's here and has a message for you." Instead, I talked to him for a while and he finally said, "Everything you are saying reminds me so much of what my Dad would have said." I was really respectful of boundaries like that. I didn't say, "Oh, I'm a psychic." If someone says to me, "Oh wow, you are psychic," I'll tell them I am. I don't charge that person because I've been sent to *them*. But if someone comes to me and asks me to give him psychic information, I'll charge them. This is something I've trained over a period of years for to really refine my gift. That's absolutely fair to charge them.

A.A.: What is your business plan?

J.G.: My goal isn't really to work one on one all of the time. My passion is teaching people how to do it for themselves through doing workshops and having products to support them.

A.A.: Tell me a little bit about the sales and marketing of your business. In ways, it is easier to sell an actual product than it is to sell advice.

J.G.: None of it is easy. Especially coming from England where people are more modest, you tend to talk everything down, and if you have a skill or a talent you don't show it. I had to learn coming out here in the U.S. that you really have to sing your own praises. For me, it's always been easier to promote other people. I've been in journalism and marketing, but for myself I really struggled. I had trouble with my self esteem with that. Then I realized that I had to look at my goals and talents and know that this is what I'm good at and how it can be a benefit to you. Now I've come to a point where I can accept that I must market myself. Now I'm launching my marketing and asking things like, how do I serve others, and what do I have to offer that they want?

A.A.: A friend of ours would call that doing business from a place of love and abundance.

J.G.: Absolutely. There's a lot of free information that I'm giving out, so it has lots of different levels. For some people who can't afford my services, I give some great information for free. Some people want a more personalized experience. I charge more for that. I love to give workshops. That is definitely the most fun.

A.A.: I can tell. You kind of light up about that one…

J.G.: I like TV too. When people see you on TV, you are thought of as an authority and it's easier to share principles.

A.A.: Is most of your clientele Hollywood industry types?

J.G.: I'd say about sixty percent to seventy percent of my clients are Hollywood personnel, producers, directors, writers. But then I also work with people who are in health and wellness, all kinds of doctors, people in the financial industry, legal people, you name it.

A.A.: Are they repeat customers?

J.G.: Yes. Ninety-five percent of my clients are referred to me. I almost only have worked by referral. I've never advertised, so I'll be very interested to see what happens as I launch my new website.

A.A.: I've noticed over twenty-five years in my industry that it's a lot easier to work with referrals. You really have to educate someone who comes to you cold about what you do. But the website gives you some authority and educates new clients before they come to you.

J.G.: Absolutely. If I want to find out about someone before I go and see them, I'll research them on the Internet first. On my website I have over a hundred testimonials about my readings. I'll tell you something else: I've really learned to say no to the people I don't want to work with, like the person who is always trying to prove me wrong. I don't want to work with them.

A.A.: Me either!

J.G.: But I think sales and marketing is crucial. This is the problem.

This is why so many psychics are broke! They have no understanding of how to live in the world. They haven't had a lesson yet that I learned the hard way which is you have bills to pay and people are depending on you. You can't use the excuse of a channeled message to let you off the hook! It's not okay.

A.A.: It's not just psychics, it's a lot of creative people.

J.G.: I think it is brilliant that you are doing this book. I've seen this gap for quite a while. Some people think it is really uncool to be responsible, but it's really fear, isn't it? They don't know how to deal with money. They don't feel good enough, but really it isn't that difficult. Really, they have to start.

A.A.: We are suggesting that we could have a new Renaissance if artists could become financially independent.

J.G.: Yes, there is this whole image of the starving artists, guys who back in the day suffered for their art and today could have been billionaires. One other example I'll give you is a filmmaker I know. He did a wonderful job and won awards at all the film festivals but he made such a mess of things financially. I told him all the different things he could do for marketing. He was above it all and didn't want anything to do with marketing. He spent two years and blood, sweat, and tears on the creation. Now he wants to just hand it off to be someone else when he should just follow it through. I use the analogy of the tortoise and the hare. People just need to follow through, but they have fear and they get overwhelmed.

A.A.: Are you good with money?

J.G.: I AM good with money. I was when I was younger and then I went through that spiritual thing. Now I am good with it again. It's like credit cards: it's one thing if you need a credit card to establish a business, but know the credit terms, have a cash flow analysis, and just take care of your finances.

A.A.: Let me wrap this up. I don't want to take too much of your time. Can you do this on demand? And does getting paid to do it affect your clarity?

J.G.: I can do readings on demand, but it depends on how I structure my day. This is what I'm trying to move away from, when someone calls and needs me right now. I can do it anywhere, just sitting in the car, but I'm trying to create more structure in my day and really use my time as effectively as possible. Having money attached to it shows that there is a value to what I do. I still work on my skill every day. I see your book being fabulous. Tell people that *you are being spiritual when you are being responsible.*

THE NEW RENAISSANCE

And God stepped out on space,
And he looked around and said:
I'm lonely -
I'll make me a world.

- "THE CREATION" JAMES WELDON JOHNSON, *God's Trombones, 1927*

YOU ARE THE MEDICI

CHAPTER 6: My friend Shayla Roberts has a knack for saying little things that knock me backwards. She is a very creative person who works with other creative people. We were talking about creativity and money and artists some day learning to be good with money when she dropped the possibility that a modern day Renaissance might result. "Wow!" was all I could muster. Have you had a "Wow!" moment lately? You know, when everything from that point forward is seen in a different light? That's what I had: a vision into what a financially successful art community might accomplish. It's a pretty cool fantasy—try it, you'll like it!

We have more media, more outlets for creativity and more places to sell our work, thanks to technology and modern communication, than at anytime in the history of the world. A painter in Lake George can show his work in the Ukraine, the poet in the Ukraine can be read in New Zealand, and the Hobbits in New Zealand can make a major motion picture. We lack patrons, at least one for each of us, but so did Renaissance artists. For every Michelangelo, how many undiscovered artists settled for work in other trades? The lucky ones worked as assistants to the great masters, but they weren't all lucky. We can be lucky. We can be our own sponsors for some projects and we can find patrons for others. It takes a shift in thinking. I want to tell you what I think it is. We are lucky by living at this great point in history. The confluence of modern technology and our global economy is poised to reward you.

THE UNIVERSE IS LIMITLESS

The secret, if I may borrow a term, is to believe in abundance. There is a lot of discussion right now about The Law of Attraction, about attracting into your life whatever you focus on, about placing your order with the Cosmos, about getting back what you put out there. You know, positive thinking on steroids. Wayne Dyer, Deepak Chopra, and the teachers in the movie, *The Secret,* talk about this subject with more eloquence and grace than I could, but I need to tell you: I believe.

When the Opera (the wealthy tradesmen) in Florence bought the land for the great cathedral and commissioned work to begin, the plans included a duomo, a great dome of such size that the technology to build it did not and would not exist for 200 years! But build they did, until a petulant and suspicious genius, Brunelleschi, came along. Work proceeded on the great cathedral with the knowledge that God would send them that technology when the time was right. He did. Today, Brunelleschi's dome still stands as one of man's greatest achievements. The Florentines had a dream, a plan beyond human capability of the day, and almost two centuries before the man to fulfill the plan was *even born,* they took action.

In relation to you and your art, there are many lessons to be learned from the Florentines, but the most important are these: they believed and they took action. The secret, the Law of Attraction, works best when you move with the knowledge and confidence that you will achieve your goal. The Universe responds to action. If the Opera had decided to wait until the right technology came along or until the right artist came along, or had they decided to build the cathedral without the great dome, do you think there is any chance the Universe would have provided Brunelleschi? I don't. I firmly, unequivocally don't. I shout from the rooftops, I DON'T! The Universe rewards action.

"You can pray for anything and if you believe you have it, it is yours."

- Mark *12:24*

Look, there is a lot of discussion and commotion right now about *The Secret* and about the Power of Intention. It's become something of a fad to talk about all this stuff and very lucrative to write about it. But you know this in your heart already. *Passionate People*, yes: You already have that fire, that determination, the certainty that if you build it, they will come. Do you think that creative urge, the one you can't ignore, the one that won't let you sleep, is keeping you up all night for no particular reason? You know it's a call to greatness! So let's acknowledge it, let's focus, and let's figure out how to act on it. If money is getting in your way, GET OVER YOURSELF! You've got work to do. You have things to accomplish and we need you.

COME AS YOU'LL BE IN FIVE YEARS

My mentor is Jack Canfield, a teacher in the movie, *The Secret,* and the co-creator of the *Chicken Soup for the Soul* franchise. I attended a party with Jack themed "Come as You'll Be in Five Years." I didn't want to attend this party, I must confess. It was a little more "out there" than I though I could handle. But I went and I am so happy that I did. The concept was this: the calendar was turned forward and everyone at the party projected themselves five years into the future. We told each other what we had been doing and what we had accomplished. At first conversations were awkward, but, if you were just a little playful, you started to have a lot of fun with it. By the end of the evening, you were having a blast! We were bragging about our bestsellers, our Oscars, and the charitable work we were able to do. People described their new spouses, their children, and their villas in Europe. Good fun was had by all, but something funny happened after the party.

The next day, I noticed that my brain had become comfortable with the "lies" I had been telling the night before—it wanted to believe them. I realized that I *could* accomplish wonderful things. The only barrier to my success was me! In fact, the genius of Jack's self esteem building exercises like this one is this: your brain doesn't know the difference between what you have imagined and what you have actually experienced. So reprogramming your brain to believe that abundance is in your life, that you can tap into it, is something that you should be able to do. After that party I found myself moving with new-found enthusiasm toward my five year goals, and the weird thing was that the right person and the right idea always seemed to be available to me. I call it living in grace, but that's just because of my religious tradition. You might call it Karma, the secret, coincidence, or a series of very good days.

YOU ARE THE ECONOMY

When I was a mere child, a president said, "What's good for General Motors is good for America." We were a manufacturing economy, making and selling stuff was our business. Today, ideas are the products that make the financial world go around. The New Renaissance is about the concept of self-sustaining artists using their talent and energy to create more than has ever been created in the history of man. In a society like ours, where the factory jobs are being handled by robots, where the Internet is commoditizing every other job and service available, opportunity has never been greater for people who create. Computer programmers are working on Artificial Intelligence, but no computer will ever replace an artist.

Artistic and creative enterprises have become our major industry and combined with the growth in new technology are responsible for the creation of almost all new industry. The street musician is only a step away from the Internet guru. They are linked by their ability to create. The street musician is a Go Daddy account, a webpage, and an ISP away from having people all over the world toss coins into his virtual violin case.

UNLOCKING THE DOOR

One of the things I've found in working with people who fulfill themselves artistically is that money isn't an issue with them. It's kind of like this: the guy who has to dig holes for a living really hates to go dig holes every day. There is not a lot of creativity involved in digging holes. He isn't being stimulated artistically by the hole digging process, and his hole is probably not going to make the *New York Times* Bestseller List. Money becomes a tool to help him to either get out of the hole- digging business or to at least buy tools to help him dig holes more easily. (A shovel would be a good start.) He is probably interested in his 401(k) or his Hole Diggers Union Pension Plan because that's his long-term ticket out of the job he hates.

The successful artist is so at peace, so in tune with the source of her creativity and so involved with her work that money is an intrusion, a reminder that there is a big world of grown ups out there that she doesn't want to join. Who wants to look at a 401(k) when she has dolphins to play with and the opportunity to perform in shows with acrobats, parrots, and killer whales?

The Affluent Artist™ in you is someone who can grasp the possibility that money is a complement to your creativity, not a limitation. We are on the verge of a new Renaissance because we are at a unique crossroads of technology and capitalism. An artist who can find a market for his product, who becomes someone who is comfortable with the basics of money is a very powerful person indeed. A community of artists who band together to support new artists, work together for a common good and to solve social problems is a creative, social, and political force to be reckoned with. An army of DaVinci's who are not stifled by the need to find a patron is an exciting and powerful prospect that any romantic would find hard to resist. *Are you in?*

Do you believe? Are you ready to add your creation to the catalogue of man's achievements? Do you believe that the same Universe that helps you create, that place where you go to find your art, is limitless? Are you ready to take a chance that maybe, just maybe, you don't have any restrictions? That it's possible that you can accomplish whatever you want? You should know that money is just one more thing you have to spend a few brain cells on. Having another arrow in your quiver such as a good solid grasp of the basic tenants of capitalism is perhaps the only key you need to unlock your potential.

We're going to talk a lot about the Affluent Artist™, the person who has merged his creativity and his career with some basic financial life to lead a more fulfilling and successful life. We're alluding to a certain responsibility, a certain stewardship that comes with your creative gift, a gift you have to nurture and care for. You can be an artist and a patron of the arts. You can be a student and a teacher. I believe you have the talent, intelligence and capacity to make a difference in the world.

THE AFFLUENT SHOW DIRECTOR

My trail of interviews in researching the Affluent Artist™ led me to Chase Senge, an independent show director who also has roots in the Disney Corporation. (Living in Central Florida, it isn't that difficult to meet creative people with Disney roots.) My talk with him was not only informative but inspirational, and I want to share it with you. Chase has so much insight into the life of creative people. His story is one of over-coming adversity. He is particularly instructive when he talks about using money as an integral aspect of show design. I did many interviews in my research, but no one seemed to capture the creative spirit the way Chase did.

A.A.: What is it that has allowed you to have a successful career in entertainment?

C.S.: Well, there are so few of us. I've been extremely fortunate in an industry with a ninety-five percent plus failure rate for people staying in it and earning a living throughout their lifetime. It's hard! There are very few of us that are around and at least working artists in this category. We are not the Spielbergs of the world and not the starving artists. We are somewhere in between. We are like that character actor that you've seen many times but you don't know his name. We are working, but you probably don't know us.

A.A.: Tell me about an artist's career path and money.

C.S.: Well, your career as an artist goes through many phrases. When you begin, you pretty much work anywhere somebody will give you an opportunity to. Those places usually don't have much money, if any. So you are in a position creatively to have to invent with nothing to work with. Some black fabric, a couple of coffee cans with light bulbs, and your imagination are all you have. When that's all you have, your imagination becomes the key tool. I've worked in situations with no level of technical support and a combination of talent levels, some very gifted, some very wannabe. You have to engage your imagination. Then as your career progresses, you make a transition to a place where you have theaters that have regular operating budgets.

The shows have a decent level of support, either by audience or by private funding. You are still very wary of every cent you spend on a show. Sometimes the level of money, being in the mid-range there, makes it more complex. You have to be truly creative to manage what you have. My option, when in those situations, is that I don't try to stretch every dollar on the stage. I prefer to use the money in very limited and very effective ways. In essence, put the performer in one great costume that says a lot about their character, about the time period, their setting, their mental state, the time of year, the time of day, any of those things and let them stand on an empty stage. That will be a lot more effective than building a whole set that says, "Depression era in Oklahoma." So that's my favorite, usually in that mid range.

When you get to a level with corporate support or an event where you have a very high level of resources, like at a Disney or last year when we did the Rose Parade, money is never out of the picture. But the difference between having to plan an entire summer stock season on less than $10,000 or being able to create a one of a kind, landmark parade for ten million dollars, well that's a whole other thing! The higher the budget is, the more you can let your creativity go on the front end. You can dream higher and bigger. You can create at a level that sometimes you are even surprised by yourself. No matter what it is, if I have $10 million to create an event, I think of $15 million worth of ideas and then back up. Most creatives are that way. When you do it on a daily basis, like I did at Disney, everyday you are working on something. In the morning you could be working on a little ribbon cutting event and in the afternoon you are working on a national TV special. You are always switching gears. Okay, you have to quantify it: How big is this event? Is it a national profile and how much money do I have to work with? Okay, then I can create within that framework. In that kind of commercial creativity, you have deadlines and obligations. You have client's needs you have to meet. Within those, I prefer them to give me a very clean frame and tell me what I've got to work with.

The hardest thing is when a client comes to me and says, "I just want you to create, go ahead! Just blue sky, give me anything you can imagine!" So I say, "Well what kind of a budget do we have?" They say, "Well, I don't really want to deal with that right now. I just want you to create." Are we talking five thousand or five million? Once they give me a number, I can create to that level. It's like a guy painting a mural. How big do you want it and where do you want it to be?

> **A.A.:** How hard is it to work with corporate money guys and remain creative? After all, they have to write the checks.

> **C.S.:** Hard! I've actually toyed with that in the last few years because the big budget projects come with a lot of pressure and more client insecurities about your creativity. When they hire you to do a big project, it's because they believe you can do it. When you go back to them with a show concept, and they get excited and hire you, it's because they believe in you. They say that this show is worth this much of an investment. But once the money starts flowing, oh boy, do the insecurities come out!

> **A.A.:** Well, their jobs are probably on the line on some level.

> **C.S.:** Sure, that the underlying theme of it all, "This better work!"

> **A.A.:** So you have to be something of a salesperson.

C.S.: I had a project where we went in a year after a similar project had been approved and abandoned. We were pitching to the executive board of a major entertainment corporation and we went in with a show concept. We had our presentation planned, down to the second. One of the things I'd heard throughout my career was when you are selling a new show, people are buying the confidence. I'd always interpreted that as: do I appear confident in the show I am presenting? What I saw in that meeting was absolute proof of this. The president of the organization said, "Last year we had a team come in and they brought us a fifteen million dollar project. We green lighted it and approved it, but we still had some concerns. After 30 days, those concerns didn't get any better. We decided to shelve it. But this year, you come to us with a twenty two million dollar project and I have all the confidence in the world that you will deliver what you say you are going to deliver. You haven't overblown to the point where I don't believe you can do it, and you haven't underbid it to the point where I wonder how you will get it done for that much money. You've hit a solid number with a solid concept and I believe it can be done. You have our confidence." I realized that the point about confidence is the level of comfort you give an executive who has to put his neck on the line.

A.A.: It's the same in my business. Most people are nowhere near as concerned about the investments or the financial plan as they are concerned that I am someone that they can trust.

C.S.: I'd agree with that. I work with a financial planner and my trust in him is more important than any number I'll read on a monthly statement.

A.A.: Can you talk a little about making the decision to make a career in the arts?

C.S.: The first time I took a drama class, I found a place that accepted me as I was and didn't put pre-conditions on it like athletics or academics did. The arts helped me to become better rounded. I did well in academics. I'm a fairly tall big guy. I had an eye condition that would not let me play contact sports, even though I was a decent athlete. I felt I didn't fit in socially with either of these groups. The first time I was involved in a live show, I found a niche where there were kids from all different social and economic backgrounds. Some of them were attractive. Some were shy. Some were extroverted, but they all had kind of a silent acceptance for each other. I hadn't experienced that before and it became a real turning point. The ability to have expression through the arts continued to take me down that path. I considered careers in architecture or as a lawyer, but both of those had other challenges that I wasn't willing to face. The career in the arts had challenges that I was eager to conquer. It was a choice of my own to always go in that direction.

A.A.: How did your parents feel about your choice?

C.S.: Well, my Dad was a Colonel in the Marine Corps. Although one might expect that they would be aggressively against it, my Dad had a "do what you need to do" kind of approach. He was very supportive. However, the first time I was in a performance where I had to wear tights, he almost walked out!

A.A.: How did you get to where you are now?

C.S.: What I do now was always my goal and along the way I had to take many different jobs that were kind of moving me in this direction. Although I wasn't creating or directing shows, I was learning the craft and the skills and the technology that it takes to create shows. So, whether I was studying performance so I could talk to performers in their language or studying design and working backstage so I could communicate with a lighting designer, I felt that every one of those steps was part of an educational process. Once I did get to direct, I could speak with every discipline in their language and communicate as effectively as possible.

I've got to say, if you are going to have a career in the arts, you are going to have to be willing to watch your peers pass you by in your twenties. You have to be willing to watch them shoot out of college and get a job with a big salary while you are still scraping by on $250 a week and trying to keep the lights on.

A.A.: That's the Starving Artist phase.

C.S.: Yea, I've kind of got a theory about the starving artist versus the corporate type artist: when I talk to students who are looking for guidance about a career in the arts, which I just did yesterday, I try and relate to them that every artist works in a different way. There is no direct path. Whether you are a nurse, a doctor or even a financial planner, there is a prescribed route to get there but an artist doesn't have this defined route. You just have to declare yourself an artist.

So I tell them: "Imagine a straight line across the chalkboard and at one end you have the starving artist. Third floor cold water walk-up flat and can't sell his work but he is passionately involved in it. This is a Hollywood cliché, but there are variations of that out there. On the other end is a person who will create anything on demand for a client, who is living at a very nice standard of life but inside feels like he has sold his soul to the devil because he has used his art for someone else's gain. If you imagine there are a hundred points on that line, every artist has a different place on that line. You have to find where how much of the passion will drive you and how much of the economics will support you. The employers of the world aren't at the starving artist end of the line. He can't sell his art. At the other end are major corporations that want to buy whatever you've got. If you are the guy who invented Cirque de Soleil, you can just give major corporations ideas. They don't even have to work and they will throw money at you! In between there are a hundred different styles of employers who need a different level of artistic integrity in exchange for the dollar. The trick is to match your place on the line with the right employer so you can work together. If you have a starving artist mentality and you go to work for a major corporation as a graphic designer, you are never going to be happy. If you can find a place where your creativity and artistic integrity match your job, you can work happily. You'll feel a lot of fulfillment in your work and earn a living. If you are constantly mismatching the two, you'll either be rich and miserable or poor and satisfied—but still poor."

A.A.: We've been trying to define the Affluent Artist™ as someone who can select his work as it pleases him because he has the financial means to say no to the jobs he doesn't want. The person is affluent artistically and financially.

C.S.: Yea, I don't want to tell you that every rich artist is miserable. We are not. Steven Spielberg is perfectly happy doing what he does. He gets to do what he wants, create what he wants and tell the stories that he wants to tell—the ones that move him—so he can move other people. There is nothing wrong with that, but he went unrecognized throughout his career until Schindler's List because the artistic side of the community thought he was too commercial. Sort of like, "nobody that good could be that artistic." Yet, when he did Schindler's List, he proved that the artistry and the craft could be combined. He hit a grand slam homerun. People said, "Oh, he is an artist!"

A.A.: Who do you create for?

C.S.: I've always created for the audience. No question. I want to tell stories that mean something to me, one way or another, and tell them to the audience on multiple planes. One of the reasons I felt such a strong alignment with the Disney Company is because of their style of telling a story that both a kid and a parent could relate to at the same time. Either way, it's the essence of a hugely democratic theater. You're not just saying, "Oh, you have to be an opera lover to come in and enjoy this". Or, "you have to love Chekov or Shakespeare to have the intellectual capacity to enjoy our artistry." The Disney style is just a way of saying, "Everybody can approach this." Unless you have an intellectual pre-disposition like this is below you, everybody can get something out of this. I want to tell both parents and children to believe in their own dreams and let them drive their choices in life. Dreams are the things in our lives that we can create.

I tell students that dreams are the part of our destiny that we can create. Once you get to high school and college, you are beginning to make your own choices in life. If there is a passionate soul inside them to do something, and everyone has told them there is no money in that or you can't do it, I've taken a point of view that I believed in my dreams myself and never let anyone else dissuade me. So it can be done. If I can do it, God knows, anybody can do it.

I have always had the willingness to take the hard knocks to reach my goal. I have also had the vision of reaching financial security while I do that. I never split the two up. I never thought I had to be poor to have my art. I was always the guy who said that my art will take me somewhere, will take me to a place of financial security, where I don't have to worry about money. All that time I spent in New York City trying to gain some experience in the business was paying dues. Work your way up. There will come a time.

> **A.A.:** When it comes to your creativity, do you believe you are gifted with something that other people don't have?

> **C.S.:** Well, I absolutely don't feel that I have ability beyond what other people have. I've never felt that. At times, when people have smacked me upside the head and said, "Not everybody can do this," I've always thought, "Yes, everybody can do this." I've considered it a gift but not so unique that someone else couldn't have it. It's something everybody has the potential to have.

I think we all come with our own set of talents. My fiancée is one of those people you've mentioned who can remember a series of dance steps she learned very easily decades ago, but give her a book full of statistics and she is lost.

> **A.A.:** Someone mentioned to me that with the advent of global communications and free markets, we might actually be at the beginning of a new renaissance; that artists can become their own sponsors and there is no limit to the creativity that will erupt everywhere.

C.S.: I think we are at the beginning of it. Look at how many programs in the last few decades have been cut from schools and how the arts have fallen out of favor. How mathematical scores have fallen behind while crime has risen. Schools that have maintained their arts programs or reinstated them aren't having nearly the challenges other schools have. Maybe it's because I'm involved and in the middle of it. I see the resurgence of independence in people who are finding opportunities to have a global reach for their art through the Internet that they never had before. On the educational side, of all the economic lessons out there, you know we have all had to learn about handling money the hard way. If there was one thing I could change it would be requiring financial instruction before students graduate from high school. By the time I am 18, I should know how a loan works, how a mortgage works, how an investment over time with compound interest works. I mean was in my thirties before I started to figure this stuff out.

I consider that a gift we can give art students: to reach for their dreams in a smart and prudent fashion. I'm not saying throw away the world. I never do. I tell kids that dreams are hard. A career in the arts takes decades of hard work, dedication and a lot of disappointment. You need to be prepared for all of it. The disappointment is the hardest one to overcome. A lot of kids dream of being the next big star, but they sit in rural Indiana, Montana, Nevada and they wait for someone to come and discover them. It takes the drive to get up and go make something happen, to take action.

The same goes for students with their financial stuff. You have to prepare them. If that little girl from Nebraska doesn't get told, "Okay, next summer you need to get yourself out of Nebraska. You have to go take this course, this course and this course back East. If they never have someone tell them what they need to do, then their dreams stand no chance of coming true. It's the same thing for financial security. We don't learn this stuff until we get older.

A.A.: We never learn things in school like how to be successful, do we?

C.S.: Well yea! The job of the local school board is to prepare me for life. I don't know that I need the third re-hashing of world history. But I do need to know how to balance my checkbook or the importance of not getting over my head in debt. You know! I came to the conclusion that most of this is not taught because most parents don't understand them. I thought I was the only schmoe in the world who was totally financially ignorant into my thirties.

A.A.: Tell me about your foundation.

C.S.: Well, there was a series of events and I wondered if the Universe was trying to tell me something. About half way through my career with Disney as a director, I was in a position to be on a very short list to go to the Disney staff on Broadway, a wonderful career opportunity. I had several interviews and I was pretty confident that if I didn't screw it up, I might be able to move to New York and really achieve the dream that I had back when I was paying my dues in New York. I was starting to have vision problems in my early forties and thought I might need to get this checked. I was told I had early cataracts. I was led to believe that this was routine surgery. Well, there was a problem and I was faced with going completely blind. I was working on a show in Argentina and facing the fact that I was going from the best sight I had in years (I've always had some trouble with my vision) to being almost blind in a foreign country. That was really a life changing event. It gave me a real personal insight into what it must be like to try to have a career in the arts when you have a disability.

Later, as I was retiring from Disney, I heard a girl in an audition booth with the most incredible voice and I said, "Oh my goodness, I've got to see who this is and find out where's she's from." I saw this girl in a wheelchair roll out and the song she had sung was, "If someone like you could love somebody like me," from the musical Jekyll and Hyde. Seeing a girl in a wheelchair sing it gave it a whole new level of importance. That was very much a turning point for me. I realized if I had been at the state visually that I am now when I was eighteen and I couldn't drive, I'd need a massive computer monitor to work. I might not have been given a chance. My likelihood of success would have been so much lower. I might not have had a Disney career to retire from.

So, I decided to turn my attention to giving back to the next generation of kids. I do it at every opportunity I have. I talk with young artists of all kinds, but my foundation is particularly dedicated to helping students with physical disabilities, who have career dreams in the arts. I want to help them become prepared by the time they finish their collegiate years to be ready to move into the workforce and have such a strong resume and wealth of experience for someone their age that their employability goes up through the roof. If you saw two candidates for a position, one with a disability, the resume of our student would far exceed the other student. In that way we could over come whatever non-intentional prejudices people have about the disabled. We are in our fifth year of operation. None of our kids have gotten into the workforce yet, but we are working towards it. One of our kids is going to graduate this year and she hopes to be a recording vocalist and work in the business side of the music business.

I've had discussions with other people who operate theatrical or arts organizations for the disabled and are interested in helping their students become self supporting working artists and members in the arts community in one way or another. We face the same challenges. A lot of the students come in wanting to be in front of the camera or on stage, but by the time they've gone through five or six years of professional or collegiate level training, they begin to figure out their own place in a particular discipline and what they are good at. As they discover all of the different careers in the arts, they settle on one. You can grow into your career in the arts without having to be on stage. As I said, it's a ninety-five percent failure rate in our industry, so we want to work with the students that have a burning passion to succeed so we can help them insure their success. When a young student has unrealistic expectations, part of our role is to bring reality to their situation. I don't ever want to crush a child's dream by saying you can't have that, but along the way, we have to be realistic. We'll quote statistics and explain how difficult the road they are traveling is and make sure they are prepared to stay associated with the arts in some capacity if their dream doesn't quite work out.

A.A.: Can you talk a little about being creative for a living?

C.S.: Yes. When you are paid to be creative, there is an expectation to be creative, just like if you were paid to be an accountant. At the end of the day, you are expected to do a job. When you are paid to be creative, you need to develop a skill. Unless you work for Disney or some other type of creative company, rarely are you given the task of being creative on demand. That's a skill I had to develop. I mean at Disney it was a baptism of fire. You come out of the theatrical world where you had a script and direction. At Disney, they hand you a blank work pad. They give you what they are looking for, a budget and set you loose. You really have nothing to work with except your own creativity.

A.A.: Do you work in teams?

C.S.: Some guys want to go off alone. Others put together anywhere from three to six people and brainstorm ideas. I usually work from what I know towards what I don't know. I'll usually go walk the area. I go look for inspiration, an idea or a message that I want the audience to walk away with. I always want a message to leave with the audience, even if it is a little twenty minute entertainment piece. I grew up near Disneyland, so I took to heart the fact that I needed to send a message to the kids who see my shows.

I was designing a show called "Disney Dreams" (playing on the Disney Cruise Line) while I was recuperating from six eye surgeries, and I was trying to figure out how I was going to do what I do if I couldn't see a performer's face or the plans or the whole stage. I just kept coming back to that belief in the power of dreams to motivate me. So the baseline story of the Disney Dreams show comes from a personal experience of mine, believing in your dreams! You can make it happen! If a kid can walk away from that show on the ship or a parent can remember a dream he used to have that got lost in the details of life, then I've done a great service to those couple thousand people that have seen the show.

A.A.: Wow, thank you so much for your time, Chase!

CARNIVAL BARKERS AND OTHER SILVER-TONGUED DEVILS

"We deal with bad checks by having
the writer fall on his sword."

CHAPTER 7: If you're lucky enough to talk to enough creative people, you find out that they're very open people. Artists talk about having their creations delivered to them by the cosmos or by God or by the Universe. Some of them won't even take credit for their creations. Unfortunately, going through life open to new ideas can be a double edge sword, especially when it comes to money. A lot of times a little knowledge is dangerous and the gut feeling that tells an investor to buy Microsoft on the way up sounds like the same voice that told you to buy that dog food delivery stock at the top of the Internet bubble. You have a certain stewardship when it comes to money, a responsibility to not blow it all on the carnival midway. Jack got magic beans for the family cow—you might not be so lucky.

For every buyer, there is a seller—someone trying to unload something to someone who thinks he is getting a deal. Self interest in the financial world is what makes that world go 'round. While we'd like every deal to be win-win, it doesn't always happen that way. You have to be very careful as a new business person. It gets very expensive to learn investment lessons with your own money! I'm going to tell you in no particular order about some investment ideas that should make your Spidey Senses tingle. Street sense is a hard thing to teach and some of these lessons were learned by someone very close to me (ahem) the hard way...

"Buy it Joe, it's going higher" Much of the investment world works on fear and greed. There is never a reason to invest in something that you don't understand because someone tells you that you are going to miss out if you don't act NOW. There is always time, always something else to buy. Don't let some salesperson make you act before you are ready. Do some homework. Ask around and find out all the reasons *not* to buy something and then weigh them against the reasons to buy it. What if you can't find a reason not to buy it? You aren't looking hard enough. Someone else is selling it for some reason.

"Free Informational Dinner Seminar" There is no free lunch and there is no free investment seminar. Dinner at Morton's for 30 strangers is not cheap and neither is the advertising to go with it. The financial guy giving you dinner is making quite an investment to give you "free" information. Hold on to your wallet and don't sign anything until you are sure it is right for you. Government regulators are getting very concerned about this particular scheme. Look, if you can't afford to buy yourself dinner at Morton's, one of these seminars just might cost you a whole lot more. Grill a nice T-Bone at home and watch a good movie. You'll have a much better evening.

"Perfect Trading Systems" Listen, there is no perfect system on Wall Street because as soon as someone figures it out, everyone uses it and the numbers don't work anymore. Day trading is a particular form of fortune telling that most people never master. It can be expensive to learn the lesson that you just don't have the gene that allows you to turn $5.95 into a million dollars. Don't waste your money on one of these "systems."

"Real Estate" A great place for savvy investors. For someone who has the experience and wisdom to know a good deal from a bad one. Running around trying to buy real estate with no money down can be an invitation to bankruptcy court. When people are cashing their IRAs to buy real estate, realize it is time to sell. The Real Estate market, we've learned lately, is not immune to the Laws of Gravity. Again, there is a buyer and a seller in every transaction, you need to understand both sides of a transaction or you have not done enough homework. Yes, fortunes are there to be made in real estate. I know lots of wealthy families who have made their money buying property. They are usually patient, long-term investors, not people trying to get rich in a big hurry.

"Work At Home" Sure, some employers are looking for people to work from home, but there are many ads that ask you to send money or encourage you to get rich by opening your own Internet business. Many are scams. Some of them are after your bank account information so they can "pay you." Others are just after their high start up fee. Ask some really hard questions before you write a check to one of these guys.

"Multi Level Marketing" My favorite basketball team is owned by the guy who founded Amway, so I'm not saying that multi-level marketing won't help *some* people get rich. It pays to remember that Pyramid schemes are illegal unless you sell a product (with the exception of Social Security). If a product fills a demand, if it's any good, someone like Wal*Mart will sell it to you. You won't have to call your neighbor's cousin to buy it. Wal*Mart won't try to convince you to become a distributor and won't invite you to a meeting to tell you about a great opportunity.

"Private Investors" Every so often you'll see a newspaper article about a local guy who is being sent to jail for stealing money from his clients. It's usually a guy with a financial background or with an insurance license who decided he could beat the investments he was selling legally. So he asked a few of his better clients to write him a check personally and began buying Costa Rican real estate or some other great sounding yet exotic investment. Word gets out that he is doing well and he finds many new clients because his first clients got huge checks. In truth, there were no investments. He sent a portion of the new investor's money to his original investors and pocketed the rest. Please don't write checks to individuals for investments—work with a brand name investment company!

"Interest Only Loans" I'll talk about this in detail later, but please be careful about squeezing into a home with a mortgage that is interest-only. You could end up losing your house when the loan adjusts. In general, the idea of placing your home at risk to play with your money in other places is not something most sane or wise investors would try. There are a lot of people who are anxious to sell you a big mortgage with an interest only payment and a stock portfolio to accompany it. Don't buy it, any of it.

"Credit Cards and T-Shirts" Every time you go to a sporting event, an airport or a theme park, you are invited to fill out a credit application for a free t-shirt. You have made a small mark on your credit soul, a venial sin of creditworthiness. If you have too many open lines of credit, the bank won't like it when you really need something, like a house. A bunch of open lines of credit is not a good thing.

"How Much Can You Pay a Month?" Boy, those car dealers will stretch a car loan out past the reasonable life of the vehicle to get you to sign up. If you want to confuse a car salesman, make him talk about how much he'll sell you the car for, not how much it is a month. Talk about the actual cost of owning the car, including finance charges and he'll be the one having to answer the hard questions. For fun, look at the actual cost of a car, a house, a refrigerator or anything else you want to borrow money to buy. Okay, maybe my idea of fun is a little different than yours.

TRUST

For as nasty a place as the business world can be, ninety percent of it is still based on trust. I have been on the floor of the New York Stock Exchange and I've seen millions of dollars change hands when two men made eye contact and nodded to each other. My own clients call and tell me to buy securities in their account, and I do it knowing that they'll send me a check within three days. And heck, we trust each other just driving down the road. There's a basic trust that the guy in the other lane won't veer into ours. Trust is a horrible thing to abuse.

Playing with people's emotions isn't very nice either. When the salesman in the tire store insinuates that the lower-grade tire won't stop in the rain and that you might kill your family by being cheap, ask yourself: why is he selling it then? He is playing on your fears. The commercial that says you will attract a mate if you drive a certain convertible is playing with your emotions. The Life Coach who implies family members will die if you don't use his coaching (true story) is playing with your emotions. When it comes to investments, playing with your emotions is no different than any other product. It's the American way! Classic rock, scenes of beaches, and happy, healthy independent retired people who are obviously having lots of sex (call the doctor after four hours) are all used to sell you something completely intangible. Stocks and bonds are just paper. So what is the artistic investor to do?

REMEMBER, YOU ARE DIFFERENT

I think you need to know first that to be a good investor you need to *go against the crowd.* If you can stay up all night painting, if you have actually glued the tips of your fingers back on so you can play guitar for just a few more hours (I've tried that, I heard Stevie Ray Vaughn did it but I only ended up with sticky guitar strings), or if you are willing to give everything up so that you might have a chance to sing on stage one day or do stand up then you are not someone who follows the crowd! By their nature, creative people see things differently. You are what we investors call "*contrarians*." That is actually a very cool thing to be.

Here's the thing: you have to know some of the rules of the game and how it's played before you jump in with your contrarian instincts. That's where I think a lot of artistic people create a block. It amazes me that someone who can learn a series of complicated dance steps that would make most people's heads spin (and learn them in seconds while some Russian émigré ballet teacher is yelling at them) can't seem to learn how to play with their money.

It certainly isn't a lack of ability. It's just that you're interested in other things, like say, dancing. I'm convinced that to be successful in any field you have to go at it one hundred and ten percent and sometimes you don't have anything left to do other things. That's OK. You've read this far in this book. I'm going to teach you some basic skills later on so that you'll know enough to get by with your own finances. While you were learning to paint, or write, or dance, some of us were learning the boring money stuff. It's my turn to inspire you by telling you some "Insider Secrets of the Wall Street Stars!"

A seasoned investor becomes very accommodating. He'll help other investors out. If everyone else wants to sell, he'll buy. If everyone wants to buy, he'll help them out: *he'll sell!* Your ability to spot trends, to recognize pieces that look out of place, are attributes that you share with great investors. When you recognize something has become too commonplace, develop an instinct to go the other way. The same sensitivity that tells you not to wear a fashion fad like Hip Hop clothes once it has reached all the way to Suburban white kids in the Deep South can be what tells you when it is time to bail out of a stock. I bet you were downloading music off of Napster or Share Bear way before the business world realized that the current business model of the music industry was dead. Imagine if you knew to buy Apple in time for the resulting triumph of the iPod and iTunes?

Usually when a cable TV show glorifies a guy who flips houses, you can assume that the flipping house's profits have been made. When the six o'clock news talks about how great the stock market has been doing and implies that you better hurry up and get in, you should probably think about getting out. Remember in high school when you used to walk against the traffic flow between classes just because you're a little irritated with something? That's kind of how you should invest: go against the crowd. Get "that look" from the people going the other way.

There is nothing wrong with self interest. It makes for a wonderful tapestry of life. Before you invest or spend your hard earned money, keep a little self interest at hand. Figure out what's in it for everyone involved. Get past the emotions of fear and greed and look at the actual benefits and disadvantages to *you* before you jump into an investment.

We're going to talk more about hiring some people to help you with this stuff a little later. Expertise in these areas is very easy to rent. Trust is something that has to be earned. A good financial advisor should have a little life wisdom, some education, and a very good ear. Don't invest with or accept advice from someone who doesn't listen to you, who talks down to you, or who seems to be very drunk (at least before noon). A trusted financial advisor is someone who will mentor you and care for your money.

THE EMMY WINNER

Gary Paben is a heavy hitter: a show director who has won an Emmy, directed Olympic ceremonies and Super Bowl halftime shows, and was a Senior Show Director for the Walt Disney Company. I wanted to hear what a true Affluent Artist™ had to say about creativity and money. His insights into being a professional creative person will be especially interesting to anyone who is still conflicted about mixing money and art.

G.P.: I decided somebody needed give me a job where they could fly me all over the world and I would just be able to come up with ideas and direct shows (laughing). And lo and behold, I was contacted by Disney. That started me on my journey. I had been writing plays and doing plays since I was 7 years old. But then, I found somebody to pay me (Disney). I've never really gone for the money. I've always gone for the job and how creative it would let me be. I really don't want to have any hands tied. Of course, when you work for a corporation, people make decisions because they have to. It's a big company. Now that I have my own company, it's a lot easier.

A.A.: How did Disney find out about you?

G.P.: I went out to California and did some interviews, one with Disney Studios. From there, I got a call from Disney World. At the time, I really didn't want to work in a theme park. It became a really fascinating job because I was able to do so many different things and never do the same thing. When I left Disney, I had directed the Tapestry of Nations, the Parade at Epcot, and directed the Super Bowl for the millennium 34 in Atlanta. I really got to do all the things that were very creative with somebody else paying for it and I really enjoyed it.

A.A.: One of our terms is the "Affluent Artist™," someone who gets to set his own terms for his work and doesn't work for someone who he doesn't enjoy working with.

G.P.: Yea, it's not that they're bad people. When you have a vision… It's like you don't want too many people painting the Sistine Chapel. Like with your book, you have a goal, a path you want to follow, and you don't want other people making X-es along the way. It just makes it easier. The only time I ever did anything that I had nobody else telling me what to do (other than cost, there is always the budget which is the big business in show business) was when I won an Emmy for a show because I kept true to my whole goal for it. I didn't have people who were trying to nit-pick and change it.

A.A.: So you can say that you were creating more for your audience or for yourself than for your bosses?

G.P.: Well, you always create for your audience. Otherwise, it would be pretty sad if you didn't have an audience.

A.A.: Yes it would, but I've talked with some people who just get inspiration and don't have any audience or specific job in mind.

G.P.: You know, it just depends on how much freedom you have. Sometimes they say they need it to be such-and-such a time and for this amount of money and to play to a certain audience. What would you create for it? You must have A, B, and C in your show but otherwise, go ahead. Even if you are totally on your own, I think you still have to talk about your audience. It would be pretty sad to have everything on the shelf and nobody ever see it.

A.A.: That's back to the Starving Artist type person. It all has to come together if you want to be successful.

G.P.: Most creative people that I know, and I know a LOT of creative people, don't handle that business side of their brain. I like to do all of the aspects from working with the set designer to writing lyrics with the composer to all those other things. I really don't want to be bothered with do they have their plane tickets and all of that stuff. I don't want to worry about any of that stuff.

A.A.: Where does creativity come from for you? Have you always been someone who was considered creative?

G.P.: All the way back to when I was a little kid. My Grandmother was an actress. My Mother was interested in theater. I think your frame of reference is developed by the people you are around. I was always around people who were interested in architecture, art or music so I was exposed to that all the time. It was like that Ever-Grow liquid you put on plants. It nourished my creativity.

A.A.: How about your relationship with money in that creative process? Does it hinder you?

G.P.: They always say, "Think outside the box," and that is good. In reality, you have to stay inside the box because you only have money to spend inside the box. They never give you enough money to go outside the box. What I usually do is give them more than they want so that when they take something away I am still more than happy. Most of the time people want you to do a project for X-dollars and they don't want a show for X- dollars. They want a show for ten times that. Sometimes you have to educate the client about how much things cost. Sometimes they have no idea.

A.A.: Then you have to translate that budget number down to the people who work for you. Some of them have no clue.

G.P.: Exactly. You also have to make some really wise decisions about what you think is important and what you think is going to make a project be a "must see." It's kind of like the plumbing in your house: nobody cares to see the pipes behind the walls, they just want to see what color sink you have. Most people who go to see a show are there to be entertained. They aren't looking at the stuff behind the scenes. You can be very foolish with your money if it is all behind the scenes and not where the people can see it. It varies too, like a one-time event such as a Super Bowl halftime. You aren't worried about how long the costumes will last. When you are going to do a show that lasts many years, like a show at Disney, you have to build that into how you develop it.

A.A.: What are you working on now?

G.P.: I am working on three projects but I can't talk about them because I signed those agreements. I am always working.

A.A.: Why are you always working when so many people in your field are not?

G.P.: I guess… well, for years, friends would say to me, "You need to have your own company. You need to freelance." You really think you have to be somewhere where you get a paycheck every two weeks and you get benefits. You really can't start out on your own that way when you are just getting started in your career with a family to support. So when I did retire and stop working at 58, I did not have a business card and to this very minute I do not have a computer.

A.A.: I was going to say, I couldn't find a website.

G.P.: Yes, I have two fax machines and a cell phone that is overdue to be replaced. I do not fly, I only take trains. I don't go out and solicit work. People find me. I am blessed because if I wanted work and needed work, I probably couldn't get it. It's funny, it just kind of springs out and hits you. In the kind of field I'm in, big shows, there are only so many people that do this. So there are teams of people and they know about you. If you have good friendships, which you really need to have in entertainment, if you are kind to people, they are kind to you. I refer friends all the time and they do the same for me. I have different teams for the different things I do, so I might call one of them up and say, "Hey, want to have some fun, want to drink some Sambuca?" That's what it's about. It's about talented people who want to work together because they *enjoy* it.

A.A.: What would you tell young creatives who are beginning their career about money?

G.P.: Have some kind of job that is going to pay the bills that is in the same career path that you want to be in, so you are not wasting any time. So, if you have food on the table and you are not starving, you are going to be able to write or audition or go out and do the things that you have to do without depending on other people. Be your own person.

THE CORNER OF MONEY AND ART

CHAPTER 8: "Where do money and art intersect for you?" I asked this question to all of the artists I interviewed and their answers led me to believe that there are as many money paths for creative people as there are ways to express art. For all of the opportunities there are to create, I was able to place them into four career paths. I am fairly certain you will find a little bit of yourself on every path and you probably specialize in one of them. I've noticed that creativity is not limited to people who call themselves artists, but creative people seem perfectly willing to limit themselves when it comes to money. Gaining a little bit of street smarts about money and career will help make you a more successful artist. I'm convinced you can do it!

We'll talk about the Starving Artist first (both the inner and outer Starving Artist). The important part of this phase is recognizing that you are making a choice to be starving. We'll talk about ways to become fulfilled. I'll show you some goal-setting techniques, some ways to start your own business, and ways to free up more creative time.

Next we'll talk about the Corporate Artist: that's someone who is paid to be creative or who holds a job to support creative pursuits away from the job. For many creatives, working as part of a corporate team is the only way to maximize their art. We'll tell you what you need to learn about corporate benefits and other financial realities. For those who hold a job so they can paint on the weekend, we'll talk about getting to financial independence a little sooner rather than later.

The Self-Employed Artist is successfully supporting himself through his creations. From writers to actors, the people in this category took that leap of faith and opened their own businesses, learning some basic business management skills on the fly. Some excel at the business part, others—not so much. We'll be able to give you some solid financial strategies that you can use in the running of your business, some pitfalls to avoid, and ways to make sure your business side doesn't downsize your artistic side.

The ultimate state of mind is to become an Affluent Artist™. An Affluent Artist™ may be working for himself or for someone else. The important distinction is she is working from joy and abundance and has removed the constraints that accompany financial worries. The Affluent Artist™ could be a famous performer but could just as easily be someone who is selling their art at a city festival. They have in common an understanding of money and how it can be used to help their creation. The famous singer who starts his own record label, the graphic artist who maximizes his 401(k) contribution, and the painter who sets up a profitable Internet site have all taken steps to make money and even, dare we say, PROFIT.

The Affluent Artist™ is not always financially independent, but he has a plan to get there. Even the financially independent artist knows that he has to be attuned to sources of funds for some of his projects: the big movie, the colossal artwork, the Broadway show. His comfort level with money allows him to think big, to put himself in a position to be making big deals, and to do so by using other people's money. He is aware that other people's money comes with strings attached. He needs to be able to talk money lingo. (Bankers and artists can have some very enjoyable and profitable conversations if they are speaking the same language.) We'll talk about some financial strategies involving tax planning, trusts, and making sure that you can leave your money to the people and charities that should get it. If you are already an Affluent Artist™, I'm going to point out some things that may not have occurred to you, but once you think about them, you'll realize where you'll need to take action.

So, dip, skim and speed-read all of these sections in any order you like. I didn't necessarily write them as a series of logical steps in the career of an artist. Most creative careers don't run on a track anyway. In each section I'll give you some tips and pointers of a financial and even personal development nature.

Really, this money stuff isn't that hard. You can learn enough to start down the path and then hire the right experts when you get stuck. I want you to *at least* know enough to understand when that happens, when you are stuck. You need to know when a "can't miss" deal is one to miss, when the IRS might be visiting, and what some of the more basic opportunities and pitfalls are. Mainly you just have to learn a few new concepts and terms, and to stop letting your eyes roll back in your head when any financial term is mentioned. Okay, my creative children, first we are going to make a Money Collage. Get out the cupcake liners, the empty Clorox bottle, and the wood burning kit…

AN INVITATION TO ABUNDANCE

CHAPTER 9: Do you have talks with the Almighty? Author Neale Donald Walsch does. If you are familiar with his work, *Conversations with God,* you know that God talks back to Neale. It began when Neale, at a dangerously low point in life, scribbled his frustrations on a sheet of lined paper in the form of questions to God. He found himself writing *answers* to these questions and they were coming from a place that he could only identify as God! The first answer was, "Are you just venting or do you want answers?" To his readers, Walsch's series of books and tapes has opened up the possibility that God *will* talk to us. Walsch doesn't claim to be a prophet or someone who has an exclusive connection with the Almighty. He believes that all of us have the ability to communicate with the Creator. But we have to *listen* for answers.

When I interviewed creative people for this book, I ask for the source of their inspiration. Without exception, they credited it to a Higher Power. I believe that the source from which you draw your creative energy can also help

109

you financially. Don't limit your creativity to art. You have the tools to create wealth and financial independence as well.

Walsch's work is essentially non-denominational. The God he talks with is very personal. If you are open to any form of deity (or even a collective unconscious) you can open up this wonderful dialogue with only a little effort. My experience with this concept has been life changing: my religious background made the concept that God would have the time or interest to talk to me difficult to get my arms around. The conversations I have now with God are relaxing, guiding, loving, and even hilarious. (The God I know makes me laugh, roots for my success, understands my weaknesses, and considers me his perfect creation.)

Even if you are a non-believer, if talking to God is not possible because there is no God, that's OK. Think of it as tapping into your creativity or the collective unconscious. No matter how you get to this place, through relaxation and meditation, through prayer, or through walks on the beach, being open to an inner dialogue and a peaceful understanding and forgiveness is one of life's blessings. You might think of it as letting your unconscious side come out and play.

I WAS ASKED TO INVITE YOU

I knew I needed to tell you something else in Part One of *The Affluent Artist*™ but I really didn't know what to say or why. So I listened to a (legally) downloaded CD from Steven Halpern called *Effortless Relaxation* and went to bed. Halpern's music gets me quiet enough to begin my dialogue. I asked God what I needed to tell you, and I kept hearing and seeing the word "Invitation." I focused on the word some more and I realized what I had to do was open the door and invite you in!

Abundance is waiting for you: you deserve it, you have earned it, and you can have it. There is no need to starve your inner or outer artist—you can have both financial and creative success. I began writing this book with the idea that some people were wired to have one or the other, but I now believe that you are the sum of your choices. You may choose to have both. All you have to do is welcome them.

YOU KNOW SOMEONE IN THE BUSINESS

God told me that He is especially fond of creators: after all, that is *His* line of work! The message I received is that all creation is inspired. Everyone who creates is a conduit: their work is going through them, not by them. Creation always involves some kind of miracle, whether you have created a beautiful baby or the first bread slicer (Get it... better than sliced bread? Sigh, never mind. I guess not *all* of these are inspired.) The concept that you, as a conduit, are supposed to starve somehow, that you are not entitled to abundance is strictly your own limited thinking. My message, my invitation, is to ask you to stretch past your self-imposed limits.

IN THIS CORNER

Not too many years ago I told a client my view of life and work. I told her that I envisioned myself in a harness beneath a helicopter that was flying over a series of corrals, each next to an Old West saloon. For no particular reason, at a random spot, the helicopter drops me through the saloon's roof and into the middle of an old-fashioned Hollywood bar brawl. It's the one with thrown chairs and bottles, stuntmen flying through plate glass windows, the piano player playing all the while, and no one really getting hurt. My job is to fight my way through the barroom and into the corral. I quickly decide that the whole point of the exercise is to fight fiercely but fairly: by the rules, whatever that means. Good guys don't hit someone from behind, or hit a woman, all of that stuff. About the time I fight my way through and make it to the empty corral, I hear the helicopter again as the harness pulls me skyward. I'm headed to the next saloon and the next fight.

I used to pride myself on being a fighter, on being street tough and earning everything I had. I had financial successes and I had a divorce. I had a chip on my shoulder, and I was operating out of fear, out of lack. I worried every month about making my income goals and I focused on the consequences if I didn't. Life was a series of fights because that was what I was looking for. Sure, I was fighting for my clients or for my family, but I was a fighter, wasn't I? Fighters find fights. Fear was my motivation, bravado my signature.

When you live like this, creativity is not even a consideration. Survival is. You don't take unnecessary chances when you are in survival mode. You are afraid to meet new people, you don't want to look foolish if you put yourself out there, and you are more worried about keeping what little you have. You are not interested in exploring new possibilities. *You believe that abundance and achievement only come if you work real hard. They are not your right as a child of an abundant Universe.*

You find yourself worrying so much about what you *might not have* that you don't imagine the effortless abundance that is there for you to claim. Yes, you could become financially successful with this narrow, closed approach to life. Many people have. When you leverage yourself by plugging into the good the world can do for you, when you are willing to release control and let the Universe take you where you are destined, you find yourself reaching new heights and enjoying the ride! It is easier to be one with the world if you are open to it. You aren't open to it if you are mentally inside your barricaded home with a shotgun, intent on protecting what you have. That's how I was approaching life. It was only when I learned to open up to the world, to people, to the Universe and to God that I could emerge from survival mode.

If money blocks your creativity, if it inhibits you, I understand because I was there. I was so busy doing my lone wolf version of Scarlett O'Hara, "As God as my witness, I promise I'll never go hungry again" that money became my master. I wasn't a miser, by any means, and I wasn't one of those guys that only thought about finance. No, it was more subtle. I had defined my perimeter. I was guarding my family and my clients, and I left little room for anyone else to get in.

LUKE, TRUST THE FORCE

Fortunately, I have learned there is more to life than fear and fighting. I have come to trust that no one has set limits on me, that I can build an even bigger and more successful life if I come to the world from a place of love and abundance. I have a new view of the helicopter ride: I believe that the helicopter drops you through the skylight and you can end the fight. You can buy the house a round, give the bully a hug or tell him a few jokes. I think your new friends in the bar will refer you to their friend's bar where you can be even more effective. I don't think you'll always end up holding hands and singing "We Are the World" but I think there are a lot more win-win situations out there than I was previously willing to admit. I am learning that fighting isn't my only option.

Somewhere along the way the switch was flipped and the light went off. Reading people like Wayne Dyer, Deepak Chopra, and Jack Canfield helped.

Getting a little older and wiser didn't hurt either. I finally figured out that the world is not aligned against me, and that I don't have to *seize* my dreams. I could just dream them. Living in the spirit of intention has helped bigger dreams and bigger realities come my way. I'm not completely there yet. I'm still a student of life and I expect I always will be, but I do know this: there is a force out there that we can all tap into. It is closer to love than to what we know as fear. I think that you, as a creative person, know about this already.

Abundance is your ally, your tool, and your right. The creations that are waiting for you can only be uncovered if you are open to the endless and boundless Universe. Your art, your creation, is waiting to be discovered by you and then by the world. The tool that is money is also waiting for you, like another color on your palette or more notes on your keyboard. Don't ignore it. The Affluent Artist™ is about knowing enough about money to let your money work for you, to stop being afraid of it, to stop ignoring it, and, in fact, to allow yourself to embrace it. There is no reason to limit yourself: find a way to let money into your life. Invite the possibility that you can create your own wealth along with everything else you create. Join the successful people who have come to terms with wealth and imagine what awaits you. You can do this. **I have it on good authority**.

PART 2: The Starving Artist

MONEY IS WORTHLESS

CHAPTER 1: I respect you. I don't think it's easy to get off the Starving Artist track. Let me say that right off the bat, I've talked to too many talented people who are committed to their art but who can't seem to make any money. I understand that you have chosen a tough road, but the word here is choice. I understand that playing your music is more important to you than getting a "real" job. In fact, I love you and admire your passion in the pursuit of your art. So, please, if the financial guy sounds too strong or abrasive in this chapter, let me apologize right now. I've made the switch the other way, from financial guy to artist, and sometimes I'm I still sound insensitive to your plight. But, a lot of this book is about finding a compromise. Artists need an audience. Finding one to appreciate you and pay for your work is the trick, isn't it? If you are doing something that isn't working, it's time to change it, wouldn't you agree?

Unless you can find a very wealthy patron, you might as well face it: you need to find someone, somewhere, who will pay for your creations.

Let me tell you a few things about money. You know, cash—the stuff lying in a dish on your dresser or wadded up in your jeans pocket—it is worthless. That's right: no value, good for nothing, you can't play a chord on it, you can maybe start a fire with it. Money is, by itself, pretty useless stuff to have lying around. It is just something we use *to communicate with one another.*

You know, I want to show you I have power and sex appeal, so I use my money to buy a car. I want to feed my family, so I tell the clerk at the Stop & Rob that his pork rinds are worth some of this paper I'm carrying around. Money is only worth something when we are willing to get rid of it. It's what we get rid of it *for* that has value. Money is an illusion that our society creates because barter is not a practical way to run an economy.

So here's the trick: all you have to do is find somebody who likes your creations enough to trade for some of their money. Now, you haven't got a lot to lose here. You have already lived without money, haven't you? You KNOW what that's like, so try it the other way. If you are willing to trade what you can create for something else you want, all you need to do is find someone who feels good about getting your creation. You either have to find a market for your product or make a product for an existing market. Get in the mindset of having money flowing to you in the same way that your creative energy does. I know, it's not that simple in real life, but at least be open to this concept!

The concept of letting money be your barrier stops now. Let's make a deal—you can do this. You don't have to quit corporate America and run off and join a commune (unless you want to), and you don't have to become a corporate button down guy if you are more comfortable in a smock. Surely, in a global economy where people are so quick to part with their money, there must be someone who will appreciate you and your gift. Let's brainstorm a little and talk about finding a track that you can run on.

GETTING THERE

Everybody talks about goals. In my view you have them already, but you might be letting very short term goals interfere with your more important long term ones. Okay? Let's go to the movies.

You and your companion decide to go to a movie, but instead of checking the movie listings on your phone or in the paper, you will just start driving, using the flow-of-traffic method of driving. You know, take the lane with the best flow, follow any old man driving with a hat on, and you'll eventually get to a theater—probably the one at the mall. The movies there aren't very interesting, so instead you decide to drive over to the art-cinema house. The picture there will already be started, so you go to Starbucks and have a grande something-or-other. Then you notice the tattoo parlor is open and you remember you've been thinking about getting a little something just for you. Your partner is really against tattoos, so you get in a great big fight—right there on the sidewalk—and he says something about your Mother, who you realize you haven't called for a while. So you do call, but she is at your uncle's watching his diabetic Chihuahua while Uncle Fred has his spine decompressed at the all-night chiropractor's. You didn't realize there was an all night chiropractor. You think, "Wow, I could use an adjustment right now!" so you drive over there. On the way, you get a flat tire and your jack is hidden under all that crap in the trunk. By the time the flat tire is changed, you're too sweaty and dirty to go anywhere so you just decide go home and watch *Top Chef* re-runs. (Is there really that *much* to know about wine, Steven?)

A simpler plan would have gone like this: *The movie is at seven at the Art House—let's go.* Your brain, traffic flow, and your partner would have taken care of the details. Some people will spend more time planning a trip to the movie with subtitles than they will spend planning their lives! There are some wonderful books, tapes, seminars and Mothers-in-law who will go on in great and boring detail about goal setting. That's not the purpose of this book, but it's not a bad idea to have a plan, especially a financial plan, is it? Once you set the goal, do five things a day towards it. That's all, it's not rocket science. (Read my mentor Jack Canfield's book, *The Success Principles,* if you want to get goal-setting right. I wouldn't have written this book without his simple yet effective rules for attaining goals and I was only kidding about the boring part)

MIATA AND HER FINANCIAL BOOT CAMPS FOR ARTISTS

In researching this book, I found a wonderful resource for you. Miata Edoga, a Los Angeles actor and Mother, runs a ten-week teleseminar series called: "Artists' Prosperity Boot Camp Intensive." It is designed to help you get organized and attract abundance into your life. A former Starving Artist herself, Miata helps artists find a way to stop waiting tables, create a profession that supports their artistic careers and learn some of the financial lessons she learned the hard way. She helps you do all kinds of stuff like budget, organize your finances, set goals and "model" those goals.

Miata agrees with me that you can't get where you need to be coming from financial stress and insecurity. Her classes include coaching, an accountability partner, a workbook, real homework, and an online forum. Taking the course will help you to put the theories in this book into practice in your life. I've talked with Miata, and I recommend you investigate her boot camps. Here's her web address: http://www.abundancebound.com

GET OFF THE COUCH

I've known some people who have real gifts but haven't the foggiest notion what to do about it. They haven't set goals or taken action. Many creative people have no idea of the value of their gift and they have no plan. They fail to recognize a possible open door or message from the Universe and act on it. The artist who thinks he might have some talent but does nothing about it is no different than someone with no talent at all. You can start small, "I'm going to paint something this weekend" or "I'm going to take a class on writing", action steps that demonstrate that you have a talent and you are going to encourage it to come out and play.

This baby-steps approach to goal setting will help you hatch a plan. As you gain confidence as an artist, you'll set artistic goals. Once you muster the courage and strength to go for it, you'll be unstoppable. Now, once the goals are established, the trick is to keep moving forward, to stay in action doing those five things every day toward your goal. It becomes a virtuous cycle—activity begetting more activity—one that builds confidence. Goals without actions are daydreams. There is nothing wrong with daydreaming, but you can live your dreams: all you have to do is buy that cosmic lottery ticket and take action.

CONFIDENCE

Let's talk about confidence. No one knows what greatness lies within you. You may not even know. Be careful who you listen to when it comes to your early-form goals. Even well-meaning people can destroy your creativity with just a little ill-considered criticism.

"I don't want you to rush this book, you don't want to regret the stuff you left out," is the kind of comment that can go two ways. It can be the excuse to shelf the project for a year or two until you have more experience, or you can think of it as the beginning outline for Book Two! Some of the people closest to you, in their attempts to be kind, will impose their own limitations on you. Don't let someone else's limits be yours. No one else has your gift. No one else has your motivation. You are the only one who has your vision.

You have to nurture and build your own confidence and set your own goals before you place yourself in a position to let someone else judge you. When you have carefully selected your goals and believe them, when you've signed on to that whole Law of Attraction thing and taken daily action, no one should deter you from your goals. Recognize helpful (but negative) comments for what they are: future content for your book. Believe that you have already created and attained your goals. No one will understand your plan the way you do, so be patient with them. Everyone will see the difference in the long run.

Decide where you are going to go with this art thing. Dream big and go for it. Set some artistic *and* monetary goals. It's ok—make money your ally in the creative process: "I am going to sell 50,000 books and make $100,000!" or "I will be financially independent in five years." The more detail you can put in your goal, the better: "I will have a $2,000,000 municipal bond portfolio, a $500,000 stock portfolio, and a paid-for home—and a paid-for boat in the lift on the Banana River south of Cocoa Beach—by noon on January 1, 2011." This is the kind of thing you and the Universe can work with. It isn't any different than making that seven o'clock movie at the art-cinema house: your brain, traffic flow, and your partner, the Universe, will take care of the rest!

OUR FAVORITE RADIO STATION

All marketing, all advertising, and all sales come down to people listening to this popular radio station: WIFM (What's in it For Me?). Understand that all money decisions come down to decisions of self-interest. You will be better able to reconcile creativity and finance. Even the most charitable person has a selfish motive when he gives: he values the feeling he gets from giving more than the feeling he gets from keeping his money—at least the amount of money that he gives. Your creation has to please, help, or profit someone more than a given amount of money does. It's no harder than that. Your job is to find these people, and agree on an amount of money that works for both of you.

If you are proud of your work—if you believe it comes from a Higher source—why not share it? You might find that folks are more enthusiastic about your work than even you. Heavens, you might actually develop a following. You'll find yourself creating things with your fans in mind, and, if you aren't careful, you'll actually become profitable! Can you do this without selling out? I think so. Otherwise, find new fans or new mediums but keep creating!

YOUR BRAND

The trick to finding the right fans for your creations is called branding. It is usually a combination of common sense and some technology. Building a website for your product and designing it with your new fan in mind is common sense. So is getting on search engines that will send people your way. Having a specialty or a "niche" is huge too.

If my kids need braces, I am going to find an orthodontist; not any old doctor. If I want to have my guitar fixed, I'm going to find a luthier, not someone who fixes trombones. If I were looking for a financial planner who understands and has a practice working with successful creative people, I might, I don't know, call the author of the book on the subject.

Even if you are multi-talented—a singer, writer, dancer, painter, and public speaker—establishing a brand helps your fans to find you. Once you star in a couple dozen movies and develop a fan base, *then* you can play the banjo on the Tonight Show! Finding your most employable or marketable creative skill is your best first step. If your brand can include more of your skills later—so much the better. Ultimately, the brand becomes you if you do it right. Jimmy Buffet started by singing in bars. Now his brand includes restaurants, a record label, and successful novels. Dolly Parton began singing on Porter Waggoner's TV show. Now she has a theme park and is able to help people throughout her native Appalachia. My favorite branding example is the author John Grisham: known for writing legal thrillers with the underdog lawyer as protagonist, he had a big hit with a book called *Playing for Pizza*. It's the lovely story of an NFL quarterback who finds himself playing sandlot football in Parma, Italy. It features no lawyers and involves no legal mystery. It's really a travelogue—a postcard from Italy. I daresay if Grisham hadn't first established himself as a brand with his legal thrillers, *Playing for Pizza* would never have reached the millions that it did.

Your brand is something people can put on a bumper sticker, a way to differentiate you from the pack. Jack Canfield will always be the *Chicken Soup for the Soul* guy, and Paul McCartney will always be a Beatle, not a Wing. Your brand will help the right people find you. Although being a brand can sound limiting, it really isn't if you have talent.

Deciding on your brand is sometimes easy. Sometimes it takes true pain and struggle. Being open to joy and abundance makes the process more fun. I can tell you from personal experience that every financial planner defines his niche as working with people who have money. At some point, though, I realized that I was drawn toward creative people who needed my help and were even seeking me out. I just had to be open to what was going on and pay attention to the signals being sent my way. My niche sort of happened while I was trying to be really good and really approachable about finance. In effect, my brand *found me* when creative people began asking me for help.

Your brand should come from authenticity. People will buy your creation because they value it and are enthusiastic about your creativity. Your brand might end up being the answer to someone's prayer. Your fans may have been looking for just what you've come up with. Your song completes their soundtrack, your painting is perfect in their foyer, or your skills are just what an employer needs to complete a contract. You have done your fans a service—you have given them something from your heart—and they have given you money. That's a good deal for everyone involved.

IT'S NOT WHAT YOU KNOW, IT'S WHO YOU KNOW!

You know it's true. You hate to admit it, but sometimes you need a little help. An established artist can come up with just about any project and then find backers and buyers simply on the strength of their brand. (How else would you explain the phenomenon that is Thomas Kincaid? Try selling pictures of sugar-coated cottages with *your* name at the bottom!) Having a network, a rolodex of people who like you and want to help you is the most powerful thing you can develop. People, in general, like to help others: you will be surprised by how many people really want to help you, if you only ask.

Building a network takes two things: people and courage. Having a pure heart and really wanting to help other people are beneficial traits to bring to the party. If you help someone, you never know how or when it will come back to you. How do you meet people to add to your network? Well, getting out of the house helps, getting invited to parties is good, and volunteering in a charity that you really and truly care about is always a good way to go. If people are something you can stand to be around, you can network.

If this is a concept that is of interest to you, I want to give you two books to follow up with. Keith Ferrazzi's *Never Eat Alone* is the definitive guide to getting help from other people. Its cover suggests "How to Build a Lifelong Community of Colleagues, Contracts, Friends and Mentors", a refreshing approach in this age of drive-by relationships. Ferrazzi makes no apologies in asking for help and introductions. Like affluence, he believes influence is something that exists in unlimited supply. One of his chapters, "Find Mentors, Find Mentees, Repeat," is especially cogent. I suggest you read the entire book for wonderful insight on becoming someone people want to help.

The mentor concept is especially interesting: find a successful artist in your field and ask if you can buy him lunch. Tell him that he is a role model and that you'd like to learn from him. Most people are flattered by this approach and will jump at the chance to help. Your new mentor may have a very busy schedule. You may have to wait a while, but be patient. A successful mentor relationship will be priceless to you—think of this as a long-term investment.

Jack Canfield and Mark Victor Hansen have written a book called *The Aladdin Factor.* It uses the analogy of Aladdin and the Magic Lamp. You remember: the genie was willing to fulfill Aladdin's wishes, but Aladdin had to ask for the things he wanted. The book's goal is to help you get over the fear of asking. I understand that asking for help can be very difficult. Think of it this way: when you ask for help with your creative career, you are asking for your art, asking for your future fans. Even if you don't believe that you are worthy of a great artist's help, remember that your source of creation is, after all, the same as his.

The best advice is to let people know what you plan to do artistically and let the word get out. You might be surprised how this works. Every interview that I had for this book was either with someone I had in my network or someone introduced to me through my network. When the word gets out that you are creating something and need help, the Universe will kick in. I am convinced of it. My experience is that the right person may just call out of the blue, or you'll have a chance introduction to someone at an event. So don't be a hermit! Get out and circulate. Tell people what you are working toward—you'll be amazed at how the world is ready to help you!

ALTERNATE REALITY: YOUR BLOG

When a Grandfather like me has his own blog, it is probably time for you to have one too! The Affluent Artist™ blog is designed to help different artists showcase their work and further the discussion of financial awareness among the creative set. For little or no cost, you can show the entire world your work and how to obtain it. Blogging gives you an opportunity to really show your heart and passion without having to go through the filter of an editor or worry about pleasing sponsors.

Blogs don't require a lot of special training or ability. You can get one started with a template site. Try www.blogger.com or http://blogdrive.com for good places to begin, and if you want to see an excellent artist's blog, look at this one: http://www.thepauper.com/diary_of_a_pauper.asp.

Once you get in the flow of being a blogger, your creativity will take over. There is no shortage of graphic art firms who can help you with web or blog design.

THE CORPORATE ARTIST: HOW CREATIVE CAN YOU BE IF MONEY IS AN ISSUE?

CHAPTER 2: Congratulations—you've figured out how to get paid to play with your art. Nice going! If you have a creative job and you work for someone other than yourself, you probably fall into the category of Corporate Artist. I'm happy for you, and many people are jealous. Some Corporate Artists are thrilled with their careers, love working for their company, and realize that they could never create on as grand a scale on their own as they can in their corporate position. It is very hard to conduct a dolphin show or stage the Rose Bowl Parade in your backyard! The issues of dealing with a budget, customers, marketing, and compliance departments are facts of corporate life. Businesses, after all, are designed to make a profit. Squaring your creative side with a profit

127

motive is necessary to survival. (If I have to explain profit to you, I will, but you'll have to buy the book The Remedial Affluent Artist™.)

MY FRIEND THE DOLPHIN WRANGLER

Kelly Flaherty Clark lives in a magical world of her own creation. Everyday she gets to swim with dolphins, fly with exotic birds and perform for audiences who are often moved to tears. Her world includes Olympic divers, fearless acrobats, condors and a beautiful soundtrack. Her stage is a dolphin tank at SeaWorld in Orlando, Florida and Kelly readily admits that she has a dream job. She is a creative person who gets to play with corporate money and she was part of the team who created the new SeaWorld dolphin show, Blue Horizons.

Let me tell you a little about my friend Kelly. A fiercely proud graduate of Ohio State University, Kelly always thought of herself as more of an athlete and animal lover than as an artist. Sure, in the senior year of high school an injury forced her to miss basketball and she matter of factly waltzed into drama tryouts and earned the lead role of Dorothy in the production of the Wizard of Oz, but, otherwise, she was on track to become a veterinarian.

She was interning with a vet's practice for several years when her mentor told her to "Go get those dolphins and whales out of her system" and she got a job cleaning Shamu's stadium in SeaWorld in Ohio. Her exposure to the parks led her to a cattle call type audition with the theme park company after graduation and, to her surprise, she was hired. She told her parents, who were concerned that she was joining the circus, that she'd try this out for "6 months, maybe a year" and then head back to vet school. Twenty years later, Kelly, the mother of two, is still following her bliss she is now the Curator of the dolphin shows at Orlando's Sea World.

Kelly has found her creative side in the training of dolphins; she has won prestigious awards in her industry for training animal behaviors that many thought were impossible. I asked her if she was limited by the animal's behavior or ability and she said, "No, you are limited by your imagination." She has developed a team of trainers as lovingly as she has cared for her dolphins. Kelly believes that her performances in the theme park's shows communicates to her audience the capability and fragility of ocean mammals and the audience leaves her show with a better appreciation and even love of dolphins and whales. Kelly loves animals; her participation in the public shows allows SeaWorld to do important things like research and to save distressed animals in the wild.

The Blue Horizons show was a creative event like no other in animal training history. SeaWorld assembled a team of Broadway set and costume designers, and a Hollywood like score, along with Kelly, as the animal trainer, to develop a larger than life experience. Using elements of shows like La Nuba and O, the show is a visual and emotional delight that touches its audience; it has very little similarity to dolphin shows you have seen in the past. Blue Horizon tells the story of a girl whose imagination takes her on a journey that only SeaWorld could present. During the show you not only see dolphins in a dignified and amazing display of their power and intelligence, your imagination is captured by trained macaws, condors, professional divers, aerialists and even dancing water to give you a powerful experience that touches you in a very unexpected way.

Kelly's collaboration with the other professionals on the show design team was a wonderful experience for her creatively. Working as a team of equals, they were able to build the show from scratch, working together and helping each other increase their own expertise by offering the possibilities that only creative people can offer each other. Need to develop a special lift so that our little girl can ride on dolphins and then fly? No problem, behaviors and machinery was created, the artists worked together to achieve new standards in both animal training and theater.

Working together, for a corporation, these creative people were able to reach a new peak in creativity, something that would have been impossible without corporate money and structure. (You really can't design a dolphin show in your community pool). Sure, there was a budget and decisions had to be made in the interest of saving money, but the show was conceived, designed and produced for a corporate sponsor. The ultimate inspiration for Kelly, her love and devotion to her "babies" was given life through her show BECAUSE there was a need to sell a product to an audience. The trainers at SeaWorld understand that if the park doesn't work financially they won't have the opportunity to care for their dolphins; they have learned to reconcile creativity and money.

Kelly's own attitude about money is "I want to know that there is enough there in case I want to run to Bloomies". Her office is full of books on psychology and animal behavior, there are no financial books, and the Wall Street Journal is not something she subscribes to. SeaWorld is owned by Anneheuser Busch, so her corporate pay and benefits are good, she really doesn't worry about finance otherwise. Her attitude about personal finance is one of trust in her financial planner; she has enough on her plate between raising her two wonderful boys, Casey and Spencer and spending time with her husband Stewart, the director of SeaWorld's Discovery Cove Theme Park. Kelly has too much fun with both of her families, at home and at the park, so she really doesn't want to come out to the real world of money unless she is dragged there kicking and screaming. I can't blame her! Kelly is not a starving artist; she is a successful creative person who has found a way to earn a nice living based on her passion.

CORPORATE RAIDERS
AND OTHER OPPRESSORS OF ARTISTS

Let's see if we can't come to terms with this money stuff. Stay with me, but feel free to doodle in the margins if necessary. Making money your ally is important both in the workplace and in your personal life. Great jobs, sadly, don't last forever. People get downsized, jobs change, technology replaces people and personal stuff happens. You could find yourself looking for a job with almost no warning. The artist who can speak enough of the corporate money lingo to get by is a marketable commodity. The changes in your job today might just prepare you for a better job tomorrow. If you are able to demonstrate that not only do you know your craft, but that you can also anticipate a customer's needs and bring a job in on schedule and under budget, you are a professional who will not be out of work for long.

I suggest that you volunteer to meet your clients or end-users whenever you can. Not only is it great to get your name out there, it's good business to understand why your client has certain needs and parameters. Understanding your clients and their business is a little way to show you are on their team and a valuable player. It will also help add some much-needed humanity to what you may fear is a coldly impersonal corporate world.

CREATING YOUR OWN OPTIONS

When it comes to personal finance, using the corporate benefit package to your full advantage can be a tremendous step toward building financial independence. (That's why they call them *benefits*). Look: someone is willing to give you health insurance and a drug plan—and pay you to dance, draw, or write—that's a good thing! Your benefit package is key to helping you become *financially independent.* Having the ability to hand in your keys and go home anytime you'd like is a powerful option that working in the corporate world gives you! Don't want to relocate southeast of Fresno to manage the corporate chicken manure factory? No problem. "No thank you, I'm going home to paint in my studio over the garage. Call me when you need a consultant!"

FLY WITH OTHER EAGLES

Some stylist friends of mine exemplify the importance of a supportive creative environment. Any place where you can ask for a "number-3 cut" is not quite a Beverly Hills salon, no matter how many tattered copies of Vogue are in the waiting area. Imagine how wonderful it would be to work in a place where creativity is not only encouraged but revered, as it is in a high-end salon? One friend works in such a salon in Dallas. Tanya's talent and creativity, in combination with the right environment and the right clients, earn her over $150,000 a year. Does your environment encourage creativity or at least tolerate it? I talked with one graphic artist who shares a room with a bookkeeper and a secretary—nice people but not fellow artists. His environment is not helping his creativity. The frustration of having enormous constraints on your creativity can be overwhelming to the Corporate Artist who is not allowed the freedom to create. As a local stylist friend has found, an environment that stifles creativity can also stifle earnings.

Being based in the Orlando area, I've had the opportunity to know a number of folks who've worked in creative jobs at the Disney Corporation. Disney "Imagineers", the people charged with designing the major creative projects for the company, have been known to host open breakfast meetings where they present their latest project and ask anyone in the company, from the cafeteria ladies up, to contribute ideas to the project. No matter what your role in the company, you are encouraged to write an idea on an index card and pin it to a bulletin board. It was a true democracy when it came to ideas! The entire building was a potential source of creative ideas and no on was discouraged from playing with the big kids. Finding an environment where you are allowed to grow is crucial to your development as an artist. You might not want to take the first job offer that comes along. Perhaps you don't really want to design the newsletter at the local mobile home community, even if you do get a free shuffleboard membership.

THE PROFESSIONAL ARTIST

When it comes to getting that great creative job, finding the right circumstance may not be something that happens immediately. Getting the Corporate Artist job of your dreams means you have to have initial qualifications and then be trainable. Continuing your education through corporate training, formal education and good old experience helps you to get towards your goal. The more you know about a project, the more valuable you will become.

If your goal is to become a Broadway director, it would be a great idea to be able to view your production through the eyes of the actors, the musicians, the dancers, the sponsors and the audience. Gaining this perspective is a matter of putting in the time and sacrifice to gain this wisdom. Perhaps your current job, as frustrating as it may be, is giving you the experience that you will draw from later. Your corporation might not have the ultimate job that you want, but it probably can help you to get there.

Every project in corporate America is considered an investment. Corporations are designed to make a profit for their shareholders. Failed projects create unemployment so a corporation's business types are always going to be looking over the creative people's shoulder. Budgets are something you'll need to work with and corporate managers are not usually interested in giving control of a project to someone they don't have complete confidence in. You have a professional responsibility to be as qualified as possible. That goes without saying. You might have to be patient to get your chance to have artistic control.

Understanding how to work within a budget is not the first thing you think of when it comes to art, but the corporate professionals I talked to know that it is the first thing to look at when beginning a project. Financial types don't visualize like you. They don't understand the creative process, and they are always focused on the business reason behind the creative project. Professional artists understand this fact of life and have reputations as people who can deliver.

PROMOTABLE ARTISTS

Defining an artistic career by corporate standards can be challenging. A creative person may only have so far to go in certain corporations. (A brewery whose subsidiary runs theme parks with dolphin shows is still a beer company, you aren't like to see a dolphin trainer running the beer company one day.) Staying portable is an option for some corporate artistic paths. If you can't stay at one corporation to reach your goal, you'll need to get all the education you can before moving on. Keep in mind that being portable does not involve burning bridges. You'll find that the creative community is relatively small, that your reputation follows you wherever you go, and your ability to talk with people who you used to work with is a very practical resource.

There comes a time in every one's corporate career when money becomes a factor that forces you to make a choice. The Corporate Artist takes a special risk when it comes to money decisions. Our needy inner artist might even go along with a so called promotion because it strokes our ego. A wrong decision, no matter how much money is involved, will lead to misery if you have been forced to put your real passion in a locked box. You may reach a point where the money is good enough, your family important enough, that such a choice is worth making and that's OK! Find a hobby, get an outlet, grow your hair, wear a special bracelet, or do something to remind yourself each day that you are an artist. Give yourself permission to chase the dollars for a while. View it as an opportunity to further your art later. What's the best way to do that? You guessed it: strive for financial independence!

BECOMING YOUR OWN PATRON

Your corporate time, the time when you figured out how to get paid to create, might be viewed as an opportunity to prepare yourself financially for the day when you can become your own patron. Be familiar with things like cafeteria plans, 401(k) s, stock options, and anything else that your employer is going to give you. It's so easy to ignore this stuff, to let your personnel department or your spouse take care of it. Only you know your goals. Only you know where your art can take you. I believe that, in your soul, you do know the general direction you are meant to go. View your job as your chance to have a corporate patron who will help you to create both now *and* later. It is up to you to take advantage of your patron's generosity! Let's venture into that corporate benefit statement and see if you can figure some of it out:

401(k), 403(b): We are talking about any corporate retirement plan here. It might be a 401(k) if you work for a corporation, a 403(b) if you are a teacher, or if you work for a smaller company they might call it a SIMPLE or a SEP. No matter what they call it, know this: you can build real wealth by participating in this plan to the fullest that you possibly can.

You put money away in these plans through payroll deduction on a pre-tax basis. In English, that means you never see the money and you don't pay tax on it until you withdraw it during retirement. This is a very big deal.

The pre-tax part means that you only pay tax on the part of your money you get now. Would you like $4,000,000 at retirement? Imagine if, right out of college, we got a job with a corporation that offers a 401(k). Let's get crazy here and imagine that you work for that company for 40 years, right until the day you retire. You decide, since you are used to eating dorm food, that any paycheck is found money and elect to maximize your 401(k) contribution. If you put $15,000 a year—the current maximum someone under 50 can contribute—for 40 years and earn eight percent each year on the investment, you'll have over $4,000,000 at retirement!

If your company offers you an incentive to participate in the program by matching your contributions, it is even more powerful. Let's say you are lucky enough to work somewhere where they offer a fifty percent match on your contribution. In 40 years, the same retirement fund will be worth something like $6.3 million dollars. Don't pass on this wonderful savings opportunity. If you are putting money away pre-tax, you are already ahead by 15 to 30 percent, depending upon your tax bracket. If your company gives you a 50 percent match, you are up 65 to 80 percent before you even invest the money. This is a good thing!

Ok, Mr. Glass-Half-Empty, there are some things you should know. If you take the money out before you are 59 ½ years old, it is taxed as income and you pay a ten percent penalty. After taxes and penalties you could end up getting a little more than half of the money you plan to withdraw. Just the same, I urge you to invest in your 401(k) as soon as you can and to invest as much as you can. The bulk of the client wealth that I manage in my practice is rolled over from 401(k) plans. In my opinion, you should take advantage of this employee benefit without hesitation!

Roth 401(k): These programs are only just coming on-line as of the first edition of this book and, if anything, they are even cooler than traditional 401(k)s, in certain situations. The Roth 401(k) [named after William V. Roth Jr. (R-DE) who came up with the idea] lets you contribute money that is not pre-tax, and that *the money comes out TAX FREE!* Imagine accumulating that $6.3 million dollars and not owing any taxes!

Here are some things to know about Roth 401(k)s: they work best for younger employees who are probably in a lower tax bracket when they begin to contribute. The funds also will have more years to compound. I don't know if you have a Roth 401(k) available. Before the government figures out what a gift they've given you and decides to take it away, start investing in one as soon as your human resource department can get you the paperwork. I understand a lot of financial planning stuff is beyond boring. Think about the wonderful artistic retirement you can have by just putting some money away every paycheck, money you won't even miss!

Vesting: When you contribute money to a retirement plan, you have access to your own contributions from day one—that's the law. The matching money from the company comes with strings attached: you usually have to work from three or more years to get the company's entire match. This is done to protect your employer from having to contribute for short-term employees and give them an incentive to offer a retirement plan for their better employees.

Supplemental Saving: Mom and Aesop told you to save for a rainy day. If you are lucky enough to have a supplemental savings plan, you have the ability to save through payroll deduction, a pretty neat way to save money before you get to spend it. Unlike the 401(k), the supplemental savings plan is not pre-tax and not a retirement plan, so this is money you can use for things like down payments on homes, financing the year-long sabbatical, or paying cash for the new Harley.

Company Stock Options: If you have company stock options, your company is telling you that they love you. Stock options give you a chance to become a true partner in your company's growth. We'll talk more about this later. For now, let's understand that corporations are owned by their shareholders. Privately held corporations are usually owned by a person or a family. Publicly held corporations have many shareholders. Their shares are traded on exchanges such as the NASDAQ or NYSE. If you are given an option to buy 500 shares at $39—the "strike price"—you'd usually wait to exercise your option (buy the stock) until it is trading over $39. If the stock is trading at $45 and you exercise your 500 options to buy at $39, the company will sell the stock at $45 at the same time, and you'll pocket a nice $3,000 profit. Or you may decide to hold the stocks in your portfolio in the hope that they grow in value over time. Depending upon your plan and on the type of stock options you receive, your tax consequences and best course of action will vary.

Company Life Insurance: You probably get some life insurance for free with your employer. Your employer can give you up to $50,000 of life insurance with no tax consequences to him. The value of the insurance given to you over that amount is considered taxable income. Your benefit package might give you the option of purchasing more life insurance. Generally this is cheaper than insurance that you might buy on your own. Group insurance usually is easier to get than an individual policy. It also makes it much more likely for you to qualify for this insurance if you have health conditions when you apply through a group. The flip side is that losing your job might mean losing your insurance. We'll talk more about your life insurance needs later.

Group Dental, Disability, etc.: In general, any insurance you can get through your employer is going to be less expensive than the same insurance purchased individually. Disability insurance, in particular, is very important coverage to own. Illnesses and accidents are more likely to happen than premature death, at least as far as the actuaries are concerned. As with group life insurance, you may lose your coverage if you lose your job.

Cafeteria Plans: Your employer might offer you a smorgasbord of benefits from which to choose. A single Mom has different needs than an executive close to retirement. The cafeteria plan is a wonderful way to solve this problem. Your human resource person should be able to walk you through your choices. You might even find that you can get reimbursed for that script writing class you've been thinking about taking, or that there is assistance to help you with adopting a child.

Education: Your employer may provide a tuition reimbursement program for a degree, certificate, or professional development class. You will become a more valuable employee to them—and to any other perspective employer in the same field. There is a stick to go with this carrot, of course: usually you must take courses having to do with your job. Typically you'll also be required to stay with your company for a specified period after taking their money for your education. Don't lock yourself in if you think you're going to change jobs soon, but don't dismiss this opportunity either. Today's rapid advances in technology make it easy to become a dinosaur, and we know what happened to them. Keep up with industry trends, expand your horizons, and get smarter. Especially if someone is going to pay you to do so!

GETTING HELP

If all this is more than you can stand, there is help available. Let's talk about professionals from a few disciplines that you should turn to. An attorney friend once explained to me that his greatest enemy is "the barstool." His clients were right on track until they stopped for a drink and the guy on the next barstool gave them all kinds of free legal advice. It would take many expensive billable hours for my friend to get his clients back with the program. Your co-workers, unless you work for a benefits consulting firm, probably know enough about your benefit package to be dangerous. This stuff really takes some education to master.

An investment professional, a tax accountant, an insurance agent, and a human resources person are all people that you should consult along the way. First seek a Certified Financial Planner™ practitioner to coordinate your plan and orchestrate the other professionals on your team. Even when you are just beginning your career, a CFP® can help you decide on your 401(k) investments, the benefits you should select, and what other insurance coverage you should have.

A tax preparer, preferably a Certified Public Accountant, is probably the next team member you'll need. Consulting with the tax guy in the mall only works until you begin a real career. You'll pay more for professional help, but I think a CPA is worth the extra cost. Together, your CFP® and CPA can help you have a track to run on and be sure that you are paying the least amount of taxes possible. Both are accountable to higher professional and ethical standards than those without the letters behind their names, and this will help you to give them your trust. I advise using a separate professional for each of these disciplines. There are times when the tax consequences of an investment might outweigh the investment advantages, so having professionals from both disciplines working in your interest can be ideal.

An insurance agent is an important part of the team, especially for property and casualty insurance. Working with your other team members, he'll be able to tailor coverage to your needs. Since insurance is a competitive industry, I recommend you retain the ability to shop around for insurance. Your insurance agent then might be a team member, but he is a replaceable one if his products become too expensive. Making an insurance agent your primary financial advisor is almost never a good idea.

The attorney is brought in like a craftsman: you call him when there is specific work to be done, such as reviewing a contract or drafting a will. As a financial planner, I can't give legal advice. I can recognize when a client needs legal help and when she doesn't. A good planner should know the difference.

When legal advice is required, don't use the free Internet stuff. Find an attorney who specializes in what you need.

The team approach to investing shouldn't cost you an arm and a leg either. Your CFP® realizes that his market is competitive. His prices will be most competitive for the type of clients he specializes in. For example, if you meet a planner who specializes in estate planning for older established families, he might not be the guy to talk to about long term investment strategies when you are entering the workforce. Some planners work for a flat fee, some by the hour, some for a percentage of assets invested, and some earn a commission on the investment products they recommend. You'll have to ask these questions. A good planner's wisdom and guidance often pays for itself.

Corporate America can be a wonderful place to work. Many creative people have spent long and fulfilling careers in various corporate positions. Keep in mind: you are a valuable commodity. Education and financial independence are not only good insurance policies against unforeseen job changes, but important tools in helping you reach creative independence.

THE SELF-EMPLOYED ARTIST

CHAPTER 3: You've gone and done it: you have somehow, against your better judgment, gone off your rocker and ended up running a corporation (or a company, a partnership, or a storefront). Have you been appointed the CEO of Coca Cola? No, you are in charge of... well, you. If you own a gallery, if you are an actor, or if you have your own design firm, you are in business. Your inventory is your creative ability and anything else you can sell. You have to deal with all of the things that go along with running a business. That means revenue generation, taxes, benefits, advertising, and everything else that the owner of the local hardware store has to deal with. Nice going, Rockefeller!

Trading off a steady paycheck and corporate benefits to become your own boss has its rewards, independence, freedom of being your own boss and, well, there's being your own boss and there's...independence. Your career as an independent artist can take on many forms. There are a number of business (and common sense) principles that apply, no matter how successful you have already been. In this chapter we'll talk about some of these basic business principles and some ways to keep your creative side alive and passionate while you become a captain of industry. The trick, as I see it, is to have your money working for you, to have control over the work you do, and to have the ability to wait out lean periods. Yes, my friend, we are talking about achieving financial independence. I want to congratulate you for being bold. It takes courage to strike out on your own. It wasn't easy for me to give up the security blanket of working for someone else, but I don't regret it a bit.

HOLD ON TO THE REIGNS: SIGN YOUR OWN CHECKS!

Fame might bring fortune, but, then again, it might not. There is no shortage of celebrities who are broke. The time and passion that you have put into becoming successful at your craft doesn't necessarily make you a business whiz, although you are probably a fast learner. Some artists hire a manager to take care of all the business stuff. Delegating is good—it allows you to stay in your art. You have to know enough to keep an eye on the bank account and make sure that you retain control of your destiny. My advice is to take care of your money. Don't sign a power of attorney that lets someone make investment or business decisions for you without your approval. "I didn't know, your honor," is not a real good excuse when the bankruptcy judge starts asking questions about the electrolysis franchise you've just discovered you own in Palermo.

You have a fine line to walk between focusing on what you do well and losing control of your business. Delegate, by all means, but keep your hands in all aspects of your business—especially customer contact, no matter what your business is. No employee will be as motivated for your business to succeed as you are. It is important that you know what is being said in your name. Remember, yours is the name on the front door. The same applies to investments. If you don't understand an investment, it does not mean you are stupid. It means you should not own that investment. If someone can't explain an investment to you on about a fifth grade level, I advise that you pass. No equipment for your business and no investment with your money should be made without you understanding why you are about to take a professional or financial risk.

MAKING MONEY, WHAT A CONCEPT!

Running a business is very simple in theory: you want to take in more money than you let out. Just write this on your desk or have a banner float by on your screen every now and then. Remind yourself that you are in business to make money. Pass on the extra fancy office space until you can really afford it, don't buy fractional ownership in a private jet until you have the money, and for God's sake, *pay yourself first*. I meet so many business owners who pour their heart and soul into their business and don't save any money. They claim to be "putting it all back into the business". If you can pay the hired help, you should hire yourself! I want you to make a commitment to save ten percent of your revenue every time you get paid, and I mean every time. Make the first check you write every month to your savings plan and invest that money in your nest egg. We'll talk more about your nest egg later. You are going to have to start running your business on 90 percent of the revenues. By the way, that ten percent off the top is not your salary. That comes out of the 90 percent. The ten percent off the top is your savings plan, your owner's dividend, or your pension contribution, whatever you want to call it. If you think you can't do this, think again—you can.

If you lost a sale, a client, or a role in a movie, you would figure out a way to carry on without that revenue. In fact, you'd work hard to replace it, wouldn't you? So let's just assume that you are going to figure out how to get by without the first ten percent of your revenue. Why should you send your hard earned money off to someone else before you pay yourself? Put another way: if someone offered you $100,000 for some work, wouldn't you expect to save at least $10,000? (If not, why would you take the job?) Well, here's how you make sure you do: write that check first! Once you begin this habit, you will be surprised how quickly you can accumulate savings and how exciting it is to stride towards financial independence!

Listen—if you don't have a corporate pension plan to fall back on, then you have to treat your business like the corporate CEO treats his: you've got to get paid first! Putting everything back into the business is no way to guarantee your future financial independence. No one knows if that magic buyer is out there to make you rich when you decide to sell your business. If you can't take ten percent off the top, figure out how to be more efficient, how to institute better controls, and how to run a more profitable business. Business is probably not your favorite thing—why do it if you aren't making any money?

That ten percent revenue saving idea is a great way to get through the lean times too. Strictly speaking, you don't want to dig into your nest egg. You can spend the earnings or interest from your investments if you must. If you are in a very irregular paying business I suggest that you live below your means and set aside more than ten percent of your revenue. If you sold a really big project—your biggest ever and you knew it might not happen again for a while—you have to agree that it would be foolish to make purchases requiring you to earn as much every month, wouldn't it? Make sacrifices for your art, but keep the credit card companies out of your pocket.

TAXING

Here's a fun topic: taxes. *Pay them.* Seriously. If you are self-employed, you have to make your quarterly tax payments or you'll end up in the newspaper. This kind of publicity you don't need. I highly recommend a payroll service, even if you are only paying yourself, but especially if you have employees. Let the service figure out your withholdings and make your payments for you. Self-employed people have to pay an extra tax. Since I know your eyes are already rolling back in your head, let's just know that it exists and that a good payroll service will make sure that you've paid it.

BABY YOU CAN DRIVE MY CAR

One of the things that you might have to deal with is having people work for you and make no mistake about it, employees change the game. You now have people depending on your ability to create—people who will need to be given benefits, have taxes withheld, and who still might write that tell-all book if they're unhappy when they leave you. (Be nice to your nanny!) Employees will have to be included in most of your pension plan choices, and you will have to pay the employer share of their withholding taxes—that's the law. We often suggest that you get your employees through firms that specialize in this sort of thing. You actually lease your employees from the firm, which in turn pays their benefits, does the payroll, buys their liability insurance, and even fires them if you are too shy!

If you own a gallery or a production company or another labor-intensive type of creative business, you may find yourself becoming more of a manager and less of an artist. Some artists thrive at this part of the business. Others don't really want to be shopkeepers. Marketing, sales, cash-flow management, and all the other factors that go into running your business are functions that you can rent by hiring good people. You still have to monitor them—your name is on the door, after all. It is probably worth $10 an hour to have someone work in your gallery if you get more time to paint out of the deal.

THE AFFLUENT ARTIST™

CHAPTER 4: Reaching the Affluent Artist™ stage requires that you have some degree of financial independence. You might be producing only your own projects or, perhaps you are able to select your next project that is being produced by someone else. Independent show producers, freelance writers, actors, and many others have reached the Affluent Artist™ level. Some are famous, and some you'll never hear of. For the sake of our discussion, the Corporate or Self-Employed artist who has artistic freedom and the ability to turn down jobs that don't interest him is an Affluent Artist™ too. Financial affluence comes to some after they have retired from a long career in a corporation and to others early on in life (learning a few guitar chords and having nice eyes turns out to be a good career move). Getting a handle on the money, in either case, is key to a career's longevity. Fame may be fleeting, but real financial independence will allow your creative freedom to last longer.

Offering financial guidance to Affluent Artists™ is not really that different than talking to any other affluent client. My experience is that you have probably gotten a handle on your finances or you wouldn't be in this category (for long). Forgive me if I am too elemental here, but I want to share with you some things that I believe are important.

THE NIGHTMARE

This tale of woe is based on two actual cases. I've combined them to make the tale easier to follow. These problems could happen to anyone who doesn't pay attention and make a few plans.

Jeff and Anthony were a committed, monogamous couple. Jeff moved into Anthony's house ten years before Anthony's sudden death in a car accident. Jeff sold his own home and started splitting Anthony's mortgage payments as soon as he moved in. They placed the money from the sale of Jeff's home into a joint bank account and used the money from time to time for major purchases such as vacations, home improvements, and new vehicles. They planned to change the deed to Anthony's home so that it would reflect joint ownership. Because they were only in their forties, however, they never got around to drawing a will or doing any estate planning. The home remained in Anthony's name. This turned out to be a significant problem.

When Jeff returned home from Anthony's funeral, his possessions were stacked in the driveway. Anthony's family, who had never approved of his lifestyle (or Jeff) had taken possession of the property. They were Anthony's legal heirs. They claimed that Jeff's half of the mortgage payments were simply rent and claimed half of the joint savings account. Anthony's six-figure 401(k) account was paid to his ex-wife because he never changed the beneficiary. His corporate life insurance policy went to her as well. Jeff, Anthony's partner and the one person that Anthony wanted to inherit his money and possessions, was left alone and homeless and without legal recourse.

Do I have your attention? A little financial planning would have saved Jeff a lot of trouble in this case. A couple of beneficiary designation forms and a new deed on the house would have insured that he inherited everything. All it would have cost was a little ink. Couples that marry enjoy more inherent protection under the law. Non-traditional relationships, for same- or different-sex couples require extra financial planning. Of course even married couples need to do some estate planning. No one here, as the song says, gets out alive.

Now I'd like you to put this book down and check your beneficiary designations. Check your IRA accounts. Call the human resources department to check your pension plan and your life insurance. Unless you want the ex to inherit much of your net worth, you might need to make a few changes. I want all of my readers to live forever but, since none of us is guaranteed tomorrow, check these things *now*. Please!

There are other issues to deal with in relationships, like who gets to pull the plug, who gets the book royalties, and who owns the rights to the theme park based on your script. These are all things that are better ironed out ahead of time. A little planning can go a long way in this area. If you are part of a blended marriage with his, hers, and ours kids, there are special considerations that you'll need to discuss. We'll cover these in more detail later.

THE DREAM

Without a doubt, my favorite question to ask new clients is, "What's important to you about money?" I usually get an answer like, "Security." So I ask, "What's important about security?" Usually, my new friends look at me as if they have hired an idiot as their new financial planner. They give me the benefit of the doubt and continue to answer. I keep asking semi-obvious questions until we really get down to it. I really want to find out what their core values are. With money, you can accomplish so much. It's not a matter of being rich or poor. It's a matter of making a bigger difference in the world and a better life for your family.

What difference do you want to make? My money goals are going to be different than yours. I have different passions, different family obligations, and different ways of accomplishing my goals. The joy of attaining a degree of financial independence is that you can really pursue your own goals and dreams. If you've paid your dues, now is the time to get a payoff! Having your money in order is a vital part of attaining all of your goals. Without money, you can only contribute your time and talent. With money your time and talent can really be leveraged. We've been talking about financial independence quite a bit. Let's dig into it a little more.

THREE LEGS MAKE A GOOD STOOL

In designing a portfolio for someone who has the means to be financially independent, I usually accomplish three things: *Immediate Income, Growth of Income, and Growth.* We'll talk in more detail about portfolio construction later in the book. Let's examine these three components and how they might apply to you.

My definition of financial independence is having a nest egg—a pile of money that you never touch. You live on the income or profits generated by the nest egg, but you never dip into principal. *Never.* The income portion of the portfolio might be coming from your retirement plan, your securities, from real estate, or from a family trust. Our rule of thumb is to use as little of your nest egg as we can to generate the income you need. At the same time we focus on minimizing income taxes by utilizing tax-free investments and drawing on your tax-deferred investments last. Your nest egg can be a whole lot of money or surprisingly little, depending upon your lifestyle and expenses. The income portion is always the first thing to be addressed. You've got to eat!

The growth of income portion is the component of the plan that you may be tempted to skip over in the planning stage. You will need to provide for increases in the cost of living over time, due both to rising prices and increased expenditures on your part. We look to use investments that pay increasing dividends in this portion of the portfolio. On the expense side we seek to help you plan for paying off your home and anything else we can do to lower your expenses so you continue on in financial independence when you retire.

The growth side of the triangle is sort of your rainy day fund. You keep the money there for the big unexpected expense, or even the big expected expense. New cars, new roofs, trips to New Zealand, and most anything else that you can't pay for out of the income stream comes from the growth pile. (It is very important that you establish an annual percentage cap on what you withdraw from this pile.) The nest egg concept will work for generations if you don't draw on the principal. I've seen many people successfully retire using this simple concept.

The nest egg doesn't require separate accounts or even separate investments (although we believe it should). It only requires a yellow legal pad and a pen. You—or your advisor—need to be able to label the different parts of your portfolio according to one of these three categories and monitor them accordingly. Your biggest responsibility is on the expense side: you must live within your income parameters or you will probably run out of money. Avoiding long-term debt is an especially good strategy (as is avoiding short-term debt!) If you are still working, you can choose to use your work income to add to the nest egg or take less income from the nest egg and live off your wages. In practice, we simplify that whole investment triangle deal even more. It works like this. If you make eight percent on your money and only spend six percent, it is mathematically impossible to run out of money. Honest to God, we boil it down to something that simple.

To artists and non-artists, I have been preaching the gospel of financial independence for a long time. I congratulate you if you have reached this point. You've probably made some sacrifices to get here and kissed your share of toads. Now you should feel free to enjoy yourself. You've earned it. Your next steps should be to protect your assets. Let's briefly discuss a few things you should know about.

PSST... DO YOU HAVE PROTECTION?

The biggest risk to your wealth is bad health. If you or a family member gets sick, you can go through all of your money—no matter how much you have. Until we get some kind of national health insurance, you need to plug any gaps in your health insurance. If Medicare doesn't cover you yet (it begins for most of us at age 65), you'll need to get private insurance through your ex-employer (its called COBRA) or directly from an insurance company. You probably know this. I'm just reminding you that health insurance is not something to go without! Please be aware that even Medicare has gaps in coverage. It might be worthwhile to look at insurance to specifically cover these holes. It's available from life insurance companies that specialize in "medi-gap" policies.

The other health risk is the one that requires long term care in a nursing home or for an extended time in your home. I know, I know, you plan to take the Ernest Hemingway method out of this predicament, but you might not get the chance. A person involved in an accident or who slips into a coma might find himself in a long term health care situation that can drain all of his personal wealth. Worse yet, a spouse can be left with almost no assets because of poor planning and high medical bills. Trusts and living wills can help lessen the pain of this situation. Long Term Care Insurance can usually be purchased from big name insurance companies at reasonable rates or may be incorporated into your life insurance coverage. Medicare does not protect you in this situation, and Medicaid is only for poor people. You really don't want to qualify for Medicaid coverage.

You have another liability. Your property and casualty insurance agent will happily help you with this one. You need an umbrella. Your home and auto policies protect you to some degree if your dog bites your agent or if your kid runs your car into his girlfriend's swimming pool (don't ask). If something truly catastrophic happens (like if someone other then your agent gets bit), you may find that you don't have enough coverage or that you have gaps between the coverage that these two policies provide along with what your medical insurance covers. An umbrella policy is designed to cover these gaps and to protect all of your assets from risks that might not otherwise be covered.

Having a workable estate plan is one of the most important financial planning steps you can take. A good estate plan makes sure your money goes where you want it to go. It avoids probate (which keeps your affairs out of the newspaper), and it can significantly reduce taxes. A good will, properly drawn trusts, and life insurance are all tools to make sure your affairs are handled with dignity and that the people you want to receive your money do so. This will also minimize the amount of your money that the government gets to keep. Estate planning isn't something you put off until old age. It is something that responsible people do as soon as they have any money at all—no one is promised a tomorrow.

YOU ARE NOT ALONE

You might be one of the few people you know who has successfully built wealth through their art. Don't feel like the Lone Ranger. There are tracks for you to run on and models to follow. One of the wonderful thing about reaching this level as an artist is that you can find a way to have your wealth and have peace.

The Soul of Money by Lynne Twist is a wonderful book that will help you reconcile with money and find fulfillment in life. In it, Lynne, a global fundraiser, examines our attitudes about money and the wonderful insights revealed by how we earn it, spend it, and give it away. Remember me telling you that I ask my clients about their core values? Well, this book shines a light on those values and challenges readers to live consciously and fully in their relationship with money and to transform all aspects of their lives. Lynn's book will help you to be comfortable with money so you can create more. It will help you see what that creation can do to change the world.

Another philosophical approach to money management that I find appealing is described in the book *Seven Stages of Money Maturity*. Its author, George Kinder, is a Buddhist teacher and a Harvard trained financial planner. The book offers a revolutionary way to examine your relationship with money. Kinder takes a philosophical view of personal finance and illustrates the seven psychological stages people go through in finding a spiritual relationship with their money:

•Innocence: Not knowing anything

•Pain: Realizing that we might have to like money and work to get it

•Knowledge: Learning what to do with money—to invest, etc.

•Understanding: You gain more wisdom about greed, wealth, etc.

•Vigor: You are motivated to reach financial goals

•Vision: You focus your vigor outwards to help others

•Aloha: You reach a sense of altruism with no expectations of any kind

I find Kinder's approach particularly appealing as I get older. The stages of money maturity line up with real maturity. I feel happy when I recognize growth in myself to new levels on his scale. I have always found that looking at money in a vacuum is boring. I appreciate the fact that money, as I've said, is worthless until you do something with it. Kinder's book will change you if you have attained financial independence or even if you plan to.

The Energy of Money by Maria Nemeth, Ph.D., is another spiritual book about money that many artists find useful. It combines self-help and self-discovery with the proven methods of money mangers to help you match your beliefs and values with wealth building techniques. Maria talks about good things like abundance, focusing on money, energy, and defusing the fear of deprivation and scarcity. If you are terrified of money or of facing scarcity, this book may help you get past your fears and allow abundance into your life. If you want to feel more comfortable with money and learn to do more with your assets, *The Energy of Money* is worth picking up.

YOU, THE FOUNDATION

One of the nicest things about having a few bucks is being able to help someone else. If you have more than a few bucks—if you have a lot of bucks and a giving heart— you can accomplish many great things. Imagine having your own foundation through which money can be donated to charities in your lifetime and even after. Would you like to be able to send a check to the Red Cross after a terrible hurricane? How about having your foundation help support a new wing in your local museum? You might be surprised to learn that you can establish your own charitable foundation with minimal paperwork and expenses—often with as little as $10,000. Why would you want to do that?

A Donor Advised Fund, as this type of foundation is classified, will help you with income taxes and estate planning. It will provide a true legacy for you and the fruits of your art. The mechanics are very straightforward. You donate cash or appreciated securities to a donor advised fund with a financial institution and receive an immediate tax deduction. The money is invested in your name in a pooled account with other people who have donated to their own foundations. You'll be able to have checks sent to charities whenever you request them. You don't have to make your contributions right away. You might decide to gift a certain percentage of the fund each year or you might wait and gift it all when the spirit moves you.

The money is irrevocably given to the fund so you can't have it back. It is no longer legally considered a part of your estate and you get an immediate income tax deduction. It is a really good idea to give appreciated stock to your foundation. You won't have to pay capital gains and you'll get to deduct the entire value of the stock for income tax purposes. Another funding technique is to name the foundation the beneficiary of your insurance and retirement plans, thereby making a large contribution upon your death. Many people like the idea of putting their descendants in charge of making distributions from the foundation, feeling it will benefit them spiritually and practically (being the person who writes the checks to the local charities might make your kids popular at dinner parties). There aren't many things that can make you feel better about being successful than helping other people and the causes that you believe in. By establishing your own foundation, you can know that you have done your part in leaving the world a better place. You'll also know that you made the right decision in becoming an Affluent Artist™.

In my career, I've had the pleasure of working with a number of Affluent Artists™. Most of them are not famous. They are just creative people who have learned to take care of their money until one day it can take care of them. Making a choice to become good with money does require sacrifice, some education, and trust in others. I can tell you, it seems to be worth it. My Affluent Artist™ friends have a joy for life and are finding themselves involved in creative and altruistic projects that they never imagined when they began their creative careers. Your journey to Affluence has begun. Just begin with small steps and watch your momentum carry you to the finish line!

THE AFFLUENT CHAIR MAKERS
A Fable for Modern Times

Jack was real good with wood and had somehow settled on Adirondack chairs as his signature product. It started simply enough. His brother asked him to build a chair for him, so Jack went off to the garage one Saturday morning and started cutting. After a while, he'd made a reasonable reproduction of the chairs he'd seen on vacation. Soon he realized that he might be on to something. He spent a few weekends building chairs and sold them by placing them near the road in front of his house behind a For Sale sign. Jack's chairs came in unfinished wood. The buyers painted them or stained them when they got home. That seemed to suit everyone just fine. The $150 he got for each chair made him happy. He got to play in the garage at someone else's expense. He even had some beer money left over. He was happy to have a hobby that paid for itself, but he wondered if he was missing out on something.

Soon Jack's phone was ringing with chair orders. He realized that he needed to make some decisions about the direction his life would take. Working with wood was so much more gratifying than his job delivering soft drinks to supermarkets. Jack wondered if he could really make a living at his hobby. After all, he didn't have much of a business background. He decided to give it a run, so he sought some help.

Jack knew an old cabinetmaker—the guy who taught him his woodworking skills. He helped Jack with a business plan. Jack's mentor even loaned him some money to get started. Jack's confidence and faith grew. He rented some inexpensive workshop space and set up a rudimentary assembly line. Then he hired a few high school kids to help on a part time basis. For the first few months he sold all the chairs he could make. After a busy first year, the Adirondack chair market seemed to slow down. Jack knew he needed to do something different, but he wasn't sure whether he should seek to expand his market, make other products, lower his prices, or what. He prayed for inspiration.

Diane was an art major at the state university. Her parent's had one of Jack's chairs on their front porch. She saw the chair as a budding canvas. When she went home on break, Diane attacked it one morning with her paints. The resulting landscape, a perfect rendition of the lake in her backyard, was amazing. Everyone who came to visit remarked on how beautiful the chair looked and expressed an interest in owning one just like it. Before long, someone asked her to come over and paint one of Jack's chairs on their porch. She made $200 for an afternoon's work. She hadn't even asked for the money. Her neighbor forced it into her hand. Diane simply loved the idea of painting for someone, and the thought of making money had not even entered her mind.

Now, the story could have ended right there. Jack could have started listing his chairs on the Internet and sold them at lower and lower prices until he couldn't afford to sell them anymore. His mentor might have demanded immediate repayment of his loan, forcing Jack to go back to driving the delivery truck. Diane could have spent the $200 on music downloads and decided that she didn't want to paint chairs anymore. Yes, the story could have ended there, but then, why would I be telling it to you?

Jack first heard about this painted chair when Diane's parents purchased another one and showed him a picture of her work. A little bell went off in his head. Jack knew he had to meet Diane. At Christmas break, she came by the shop and agreed to paint five of the chairs. They brought them to the county art festival and put the "ridiculous" price of $850 on each of them. All the chairs sold that day and Jack took orders for five more. In one day he had earned more than he'd previously made in a month of selling chairs. A little paint and a lot of Diane's talent allowed him to sell the chairs for $700 more than he had before. Jack might not have had an MBA, but he knew it would be a good idea to sell more $850 chairs!

Diane didn't want to quit school to join Jack's business, but she did love the idea that someone was willing to pay for her art. They reached an agreement that she would design four new chairs on spring break and four more at the end of the summer. Jack hired craftsmen to paint the chairs with Diane's design and agreed to pay her a flat fee of $50 dollars for every chair that he sold. Even with the added cost of painting the chairs, Jack was very happy with the new arrangement. He began to sell "limited edition" chairs all over the world via the Internet. A home décor magazine found out about Diane's unique style and featured the chairs in a "Front Porch Dreams" issue. Soon it was off to the races for Jack's little chair factory!

It could have gotten ugly here, too. Jack could have frozen Diane out and hired more painters to produce chairs under his company's name. Diane could have started shopping her name around the Adirondack chair manufacturing community to find a better deal. Luckily, the two new friends liked their arrangement and just kept moving forward. Before long, the chair company required an entire building as well as full time shipping, accounting, and human resource departments. Diane's creations became a well-known brand name. At first people discovered her talent through the chair company. Now she had developed her own reputation as an artist. She was being asked to paint more than chairs. When she completed her university degree, she was able to open her own studio and it became very successful.

The income from the chair business allowed Diane to focus on creating her own art. She didn't have to worry about the bills. Her inspired work already had a market, thanks to her brand name. She already had a fan base. Jack's wood business flourished too. People knew that his work and materials were first-rate. They were willing to pay a premium for his chairs and the accompanying accent pieces he now offered.

The story could have turned ugly here too. Jack and Diane might have ignored the fundamentals of good money management and ended up drunk and bitter. They could have lived beyond their means, overextended themselves on credit, entered into marriages with irresponsible partners, and begun overproducing chairs while cutting back on quality. To clear up their debt they might have sold to a major corporation that would have fired Jack's employees, moved the manufacturing operations to Djibouti, and used Diane's brand name on bedroom slippers and mini van seat covers. They could have, but they didn't. (Hey—this is my fable—I like happy endings!)

They found a great Certified Financial Planner™ (our hero!) who helped them create budgets, got them on a savings plan, and worked with them for many years. He taught Jack and Diane the importance of living below their means and of saving ten percent of their net income. It wasn't long before they were both financially independent. They reached the point where their money could take care of them because they had taken care of it. They now worked because they cared about their work. Money was their reward for doing a great job, but not an end in itself.

Years after making that first chair, Jack finally sold his business and retired. He sold it to his employees, though, which would keep the jobs in his town for years to come. He still likes to build stuff in his garage, and he mentors young businessmen the way his old friend mentored him—life is indeed a circle. Diane's protégés are found throughout the art world and her work is now found in museums. Diane's foundation sponsors three talented art students' tuition at her alma mater every year. It will do so forever in perpetuity. Both Jack and Diane have made provisions for their families' well-being for generations to come. The proper trusts and investments have been implemented to insure their prosperity, no matter what happens to Jack or Diane.

All this happened because some financial planner asked his brother to build him an Adirondack chair! (I told you I like happy endings!) The willingness of people like Jack and Diane to incorporate business principles into the creative process is one of the things that makes the world go 'round. You are invited to join the party. Don't deprive us of your work any longer—we need you!

THE AFFLUENT ARTIST DASHBOARD™

To get off the Starving Artist Track, there are some financial things that you need to do, no matter how much you don't want to deal with them. I'm going to make this as painless as I can. I know you'd rather be playing, so let's see if we can be playful with this money stuff.

WARNING 1: The word spreadsheet is way to frightening for most mortals. I haven't come up with a better word, but a yellow piece of paper with lines is all you need and the yellow part is negotiable!)

WARNING 2: The Dashboard: Spreadsheets will suck if you let them get to you, so make this one fun. Get Excel out, use the colors, play with the graphs, or do the whole thing in watercolors on your apartment wall, whatever it takes to make them interesting to you. I want you to make a simple spreadsheet that includes all of your assets, bills, and money goals. You need to know where you are before you know how to get where you are going. If you don't have many assets, this won't take long. Do it anyway!

AFFLUET ARTIST Dashboard™

My Bank Accounts   My Monthly Bills:

My Investments

My Monthly Income

My Money Goal

I'm not saying you actually have to complete a budget. I just want you to begin by having an idea written on paper telling you with no uncertainty where you stand financially. A budget is a nice next step for some folks. Others find a budget to be an exercise in guilt and frustration (I know I do). Just knowing what is coming in and what is going out is a significant step for most creative people. Once your brain focuses on these numbers, it will come up with some solutions—that's what brains are good at.

Your money goal can be as simple as "I want $1,000 in the bank" or "I want to earn $500 a week." Just set a target and know you can always change it. This simple little Dashboard is a handy way to ease into a state of awareness about your money. Keep it on your desktop, in your wallet, or post it on your fridge. Change it any time the numbers change. Keep it alive and consult it no less than weekly. At this stage in your career, your dashboard is very simple. You can trade up to a fancier one later.

Your Dashboard entries should be no more than one line. Don't list all of your bills. Instead just total them up. If your income is irregular—dependent on commissions or tips, for example—estimate as accurately as you can. Change it weekly to keep it as realistic as possible. Having to write down a number that is low every single week will force you to focus on an area that you'll need to change. If you make new purchases, even if they are for your art or for food, keep track of them. It really won't help you to lie to yourself. Writing the goal, in my experience, is crucial. By focusing on a real number, you'll be less likely to blow extra income on pork rinds or whatever your particular temptation might be.

Keeping this dashboard up to date is a simple habit that will help you assimilate the concept of money as your ally. If you have a goal to take some time off to write, open your own business, or buy a new computer to create better graphics, having an approach to incorporate money into your planning is going to get you there faster. Once you have completed your dashboard for the week, release it. Don't let the dashboard turn into something you dread looking at, like the bathroom scale. Rather, you should find it cathartic to acknowledge your financial goals and the steps you are taking to fulfill them.

I want to invite you to have fun with your Dashboard and be as artistic as you want to be. If you need to create it with a medium that makes you happy, like watercolors or charcoal pencils, do it! If you want to use computer graphics to create a virtual Kenworth truck dashboard or re-claim an actual sports car dashboard, have fun. Let your inner artist know that you can play with this money stuff too. If you are a writer, use words to describe your numbers. You might begin with despair for your income and have a goal of reaching bliss! Perhaps you want to meditate on the dashboard before you create it. This might help to motivate you or you might find a better dashboard design. We'll talk more about the Dashboard in the Affluent Artist Method™. I hope you'll incorporate it now! Meanwhile . . .

FINANCIAL STUFF YOU NEED TO DO TODAY

Burn the Credit Cards: When you think about it, isn't it stupid that you still owe Visa for a pair of shoes you bought a year ago? I mean, really. Just between us. Is there a better word than stupid to describe the idea of borrowing money from a bank to buy an "Eat Your Honey" tee shirt at the Go Cart Track? If your bills are keeping you from following your real passion, if you have to keep waiting tables because of your car payment, then you aren't focusing on the real sacrifice an artist is supposed to be making for his art. You are getting the starving artist part wrong!

If you want to make a sacrifice for your art, start here: go without anything you have to borrow money to get. If you want to stand out, be a rebel. There is nothing more counter-culture, more un-middle class, than saying no to credit. Credit card debt in the United States is estimated to be over $735 billion dollars. The average family owes over $8,000 to their credit cards. With average interest rates over 14 percent and average annual interest payments totaling over $1,000, many American can only afford to meet the minimum payment on credit cards.

Don't be stupid! Cancel your credit cards, turn off the Home Shopping Network, and simplify in the name of creativity. If you are borrowing money to impress your friends, get new friends. With the exception of food and shelter, eliminate the phrase, "I had to have it" from your vocabulary. More crap has been purchased because someone "had to have it" than in the name of any phrase in history. *"But Hannibal, I had to have trunk-warmers for the elephants."*

I'll talk more later about the value of building good credit and the proper use of leverage and debt. For now, at this stage of your creative career, let's not dig a hole we can't climb out of. If you want to be sure that you will never, ever be able to let your creative artist come out and play, borrow on a bunch of credit cards and start making minimum payments.

Don't Be A Sucker: Don't spend money to join a work-at-home scheme or a multi-level marketing scam. Don't buy a penny stock or cash in your 401(k) to open a taxidermy and veterinary franchise (even if the motto is catchy: "Either way you get your dog back!"). Sadly, the business world is full of sharks, people who are willing to feed you half-truths, vague promises and prey on your willingness to trust them. Before you write someone a check, ask a few more questions. Consider hiring an advisor, or even ask a real smart person whose opinion you value about everything else. Common sense is a valuable commodity, especially if someone has just dazzled you with the answer to your prayers.

Develop a New Habit: Become a saver of money. Start a habit that becomes as regular as brushing your teeth. (Most people save like they floss, whenever they really are desperate or when they feel really guilty). My experience in dealing with people and their money is this: you are either good with money or you aren't. I've seen twins inherit money and one blows through it while the other builds on his inheritance. The best way to become good with money is to make it a habit to put some away every day or every week. I don't care if it is only ten dollars—put some away. I suggest having a systematic amount withdrawn from your checking account or even your paycheck. Filling in a higher number every week on your Dashboard is wonderful psychological re-enforcement as well as an important step toward your goal. Pay yourself first is the old saying, and you need to start doing it now!

PART 3

FINANCIAL STUFF YOU JUST GOTTA KNOW

"Who knew there'd be such a substantial penalty
for early withdrawal?"

IT'S A GIVEN that you don't want to become a Wall Street genius.
My goodness, you probably don't even want to read this part of my book! I

understand. I would like to take a crack at explaining some things that will come up along the way in your financial travels. I'm prepared to give you an understanding of some elementary stuff that will at least allow you to tread water when you are meeting with the head budget guy, the banker you want to give you a loan, or the financial planner you suspect might land you in hot water instead of in affluence. Remember: asking for help is a good thing, but you just *have* to know some of this stuff!

I DON'T HAVE IT BUT I WANT IT

ACT 1: Let's begin with the most basic money principle—the Rosetta Stone of business. It's a simple concept. It applies to every transaction, every project, and every investment: *supply and demand.* The more plentiful something is, the less someone is willing to pay for it. That's what makes the business world go 'round. Know this concept and you will grasp the essence of most any business and why it is a success. Sea World wouldn't be able to charge a small fortune for admission to their parks if there were a dolphin show in every mall. (By the way, they have miniature poodles. Why don't they breed miniature dolphins so we can have them in our swimming pools? I'm just saying ...) Every work of art is unique. Those who find a paying audience are tapping into the first law of supply and demand: you are supplying something so unique that people are willing to pay to have it

I grew up in New England where you can't dig a hole without hitting rock. You actually have to sift garden soil through a screen to get the rocks out.

Today I live in Florida, which is a sand bar separating the Atlantic Ocean from the Gulf of Mexico. We have lots of sand, and here people will buy rocks! They buy rocks for their yards and rocks for their patios. They even come home from trips up north with rocks as souvenirs! Now if we could just find a market for all this sand.

When do a composer's songs, a painter's paintings, or an author's words reach their highest value? That's right—when the artist assumes room temperature. Why? Two reasons: first, people remember the artist and the demand for his work increases when his obituary is in the news. Second, because it's now certain that there will be no more supply of that artist's work. This supply and demand stuff works on most everything: homes, stocks, bonds, postage stamps, antiques, art, and just about anything that exists in relatively limited supply and has the potential to appreciate in value. We call these things investments.

What Investing Is

Your car is not an investment unless you are going to run a limo service with it. A car, despite what the car dealer claims, is an expense. The same is true of your plasma TV, your Gameboy, and the cement statue of St. Joseph in your backyard from K-Mart. They are all expenses, not investments. One of the first things you need to know about money is this difference: *you can spend it or you can save it.* When you save it, you are either saving it until you spend it (like having a St. Joseph statue on layaway) or you are saving it to invest it. That's it. That's pretty much all you can do with money. Now please, put the book down and go paint. Process this one for a while: *you can only do two things with money!*

We are real, real good at the spending part. We spend money we haven't even made yet to buy stuff that will be gone, broken, or lost by the time we pay for it to impress people we don't care much about. I don't need to tell you how to do this, so let's talk a little about the other option—the saving part. Why save it? We might need more money than we currently have to buy something we want, like a car, so we save with a purpose or goal. (I have to explain this last statement to people sometimes. It is legal and practical to save money to buy something. You don't *have* to buy it now on credit.) We can have short-term goals (like purchases) or long-term goals (like financial independence). We can save a little or a lot. It is this choice that helps determine your financial security and independence.

IT'S A WONDERFUL LIFE (WHAT CAN I DO WITH MY MONEY)

ACT 2: Let's say that you decide to overcome our culture, your consumer weakness and American Express, and start to save some money. Once again, you have two choices: *you can buy something or you can loan your money to someone.* You can read a *Wall Street Journal,* open to the section with the small lines of agate type listing every investment sold in the financial markets the day before, and narrow each of them down to one of two things: *a loan or ownership.*

Let's start with the loan part of the equation, because that's what you were doing when Mom marched you down to the Building and Loan and opened a savings account for you. The nice young teller explained to you that he wouldn't keep your money here. He would lend it out to the good people of Bedford Falls to buy homes and cars and swimming pools. The important point is this: you didn't *own* the bank or the houses they helped to build. You were only loaning some money to them. In exchange, you expected to get your money back along with a little bit of interest.

When you buy a Certificate of Deposit or open a savings account or most any other kind of bank account, you are loaning your money to someone who has agreed to pay you back with interest within a certain timeframe. When you buy a bond, almost any kind of bond—Municipal, Government, Corporate, Savings, etc.—you are letting someone else use your money with the expectation of getting it back. Isn't that the essence of a loan? When you hit your father up for gas money as a teenager, you had no intention of paying him back. He knew he'd never see that money again, so that wasn't technically a loan. You will find in the real world that people very much expect to get their money back. They are actually insistent on it.

The alternative to loaning money is to *buy* something, so let's imagine that you have purchased a home financed by the Bedford Falls Building and Loan. You now own something with your money (a couple of decent rooms and a bath, to be exact). You have no guarantee that you will ever see the money you spent again. Instead, you have equity, or ownership, in your home. If your house goes down in value there is no FDIC (Federal Deposit Insurance Corporation) and no insurance company to step in to guarantee your purchase price. Upon purchase you assumed the risk that goes along with owning a home. Sometimes with risk, there is reward.

Stocks fall into the general category of ownership or equity too. Let's put it this way: suppose that you noticed the nerdy kid next door dropped out of Harvard and was playing with something called computers in the garage with his friend named Paul. The kid, little Billy, needs some money to buy some transistors, a soldering iron, and a copy of *Playboy* (don't ask), so you offer to finance him. He offers you two proposals. The first is that he will pay you back in six months plus five percent interest. The second choice sounds crazy to you: he'll give you half ownership of the new company. Your reaction is that you might never see your $29.65 loan again, so you take the first option. Nice going.

In Bill's second option, you would have owned stock in his company, with each share of stock representing part ownership. That's why we call stocks "equities" and why you buy them only because you want to build wealth. When you buy a bond, you are saying that you'd like to preserve the money you have, and you'd like a little interest for letting someone else play with your money—just like you did with Billy's new company! When you buy a stock, you expect to make money. Don't buy a stock because you like the company's logo, its advertising, its founder, its corporate spokesman, its stance on the environment, the benefit package it offers to non married couples, or even its product. If I like a company's pork rinds, I might be a customer. That doesn't mean I'm willing to be a part owner of that company. Know this: *you only buy a stock because you think someone will buy it from you at a higher price in the future.* So now you know enough to be dangerous, and you know that first question to ask before you invest in anything: *Am I an owner or am I a creditor?* Anything you do with money is simply a variation on these two themes, no matter how complicated and wonderful someone tries to make it sound.

YOU'VE GOT TO LIVE SOMEWHERE

ACT 3: Speaking of home equity, let's talk about having one. We here at the Affluent Artist™ highly recommend getting off the street and having a home. The first question, of course, is, "Should I own or rent?" We'll give that a strong, "I don't know!" in reply. I will give you a few questions to ask yourself and some arguments for either side of the equation. Many well-meaning people are locked into the idea that you must own a home to get anywhere financially. After all, home ownership is a cornerstone of the American Dream. I'm of the opinion that not all people need to assume the risk and extra expense of home ownership. The finances don't always make sense.

You are going to have to live *somewhere* and it will cost something to do so, no matter what. However, the creative lifestyle might require that you be able to move around on short notice or live with an irregular income. There are a few things that might get in your way when you own a home. Number one is *you own a home.* You'll have responsibilities and expenses over and above those you face as a renter. In addition to cleaning out the gutters, repairing leaky faucets, and killing the family of insects that decided to move in last night, you've got to save up for a new roof, pay for your own new carpet, and budget for insurance and taxes.

"But a house is such a great investment!" is the other argument. Well yes— since you have to live somewhere—home ownership is a pretty good way to pay for living somewhere, in the long run. That's why I own a home. Let's remember that the housing market is subject to the same principles of supply and demand that impact every other financial transaction. Historically, homes have appreciated in value. That doesn't mean *you* are guaranteed to purchase a home that will increase in value. Realtors love to tell you something like this, and I actually heard a real estate guy say this on the radio: "Your house will appreciate in value 15 percent a year!" So, just plug that number into your spreadsheet: buy a house for $150,000 and compound the value at 15% a year until your projected retirement age and, bingo, you have all the money you'll ever need!

Okay, let's break this down and do the math: Let's say you bought a home when you were 30 years old and paid on a 30-year mortgage until you were 60 years old. Let's compound your $150,000 purchase price at 15 percent for 30 years. My very professional, very complicated HP 10BII business calculator says your house should sell for about $9.9 million dollars in thirty years. Wow! *Please understand that your house isn't going to increase in value at 15% a year.* Are there any thirty-year-old, $9.9 million dollar houses on your street? Mine either. What if your house grew in value at 10 percent for thirty years? That still makes its imaginary sales price somewhere around $2.6 million. Unless you are Jed Clampett, this probably isn't going to happen to your home.

Supply and Demand (Again)

The fact is, supply and demand enters into the resale value of homes too. It begins with entry-level, first time home buyers. They are nearly always going to make a home buying decision based on their ability to make a monthly mortgage payment. As a result, certain neighborhoods will reach a maximum value at some point. A fixer-upper in Bedford Falls is not going to command a couple of million dollars, much less ten. It's going to go for whatever the target monthly mortgage payment works out to be. Unless the target market for the neighborhood changes, that's it. We'll talk more about interest rates and mortgages in a minute. Let's keep it simple: *people can only spend as much on a house as the bank will loan them.* The bank will only loan them as much money as it determines they can afford to repay every month. To further protect their investment, they won't loan more than they think they can resell it for if you fall into foreclosure.

Let's just say that your house might get *some* appreciation and leave it at that. Remember that the cost of living is increasing at the same time as your home's value. We'll examine the costs of a mortgage in a minute. First, let's talk about *not* financing your home. Let's say you plunked down $150,000 cash money and bought your home. You lived in it for 30 years and your home did appreciate in value. Let's say it doubled. Not a bad deal. You got to live somewhere and got twice your purchase price back. It's not a given that this is the best financial solution for you. Let's do some more math.

What if you invested that $150,000 somewhere else? What would it be worth thirty years from now? Would it be worth more than my $150,000 house after the same period of time? What about those tax, insurance, and maintenance costs? If I actually factor those into the equation (and to be fair

I should), is my house still a great investment? Suppose I invested that money instead and subtracted the cost of rent from the investment return each year? I can insert any numbers I want to make the house look like a good investment or a bad one, but that's not my point. My point: a house *might* be a good fit and it might not. You should not go along with common wisdom that might not apply to you. Consider what you've read here and do some math. Talk with your financial planner and come to the decision that's best for you.

Mortgage Madness

Understanding how a mortgage works hasn't always been as important as it is now. In the past, you went to the bank, their loan committee decided how much to lend you, then they told you how much you had to put down and how much you had to pay each month. Today you have a multitude of mortgage options. If you don't do your homework, you could end up choosing one that's bad for you and your financial well-being. Let's talk about a few things you just have to know.

The first is this: mortgages amortize. What that means is that you pay back your loan—principal and interest—over a set period of time which is agreed upon by you and the mortgage company. A conventional mortgage allows you to pay your money back over thirty years. It's important to know that in the way the schedule is set up, you pay more interest towards the beginning of the loan and more principal towards the end. Let's say you borrowed $150,000 at 6.5 percent for that house. Ten years into your 30-year mortgage, you'd still owe about $127,000 of principal. That's right, you've only paid about $13,000 back of your loan! All of your payments for ten years have been almost entirely interest to the lending institution. Remember my advice to pay yourself first? Banks do the same thing!

If you lived in your house for all 30 years of the 6.5 percent, $150,000 mortgage, you would have sent $344,876 to the bank. To reduce both the duration of your mortgage and its cost, making an extra payment a year is a good place to begin. You save almost $47,000 over the life of your loan and pay it off about *six years earlier* by sending *one* extra payment at the beginning of each year. Our payment on this mortgage is about $958 a month. Making an extra $250 payment a month is an even better savings method: we'd actually save over $91,000 and have the entire loan paid off in 17 years! The higher your interest rate, the more you save by using one of these two strategies.

The more choices there are, the more likely borrowers who haven't done their homework are to choose the wrong mortgage. They'll lock in a rate for thirty years, thinking they are being safe, even if they only plan to stay in the house for four or five years. Then the American consumer mentality kicks in, making it easy to urge us to buy as much house as we can afford—per month. Let's suppose we got past that and looked at what it really costs us to own a home? If we got the same mortgage as we just discussed, same interest rate and everything, but *lowered the term to 15 years*, we'd have a much more reasonable cost of owning a home. Our payment would be $1314 a month (only about $350 more a month than before), and we would only send the bank a total of $236,000 to own our home. We are also through doing business with the mortgage company 15 years earlier too. If we made one extra payment a year on this loan, we'd be done in 13 years and save another $11,000. When you consider that 15-year loans usually have a better interest rate, it is easy to see why it makes sense to buy a little less home and be able to see the light at the end of the tunnel! The concept of living in a home that is *paid for* is the true American dream. It's a great dream to have.

A relatively new option in the mortgage market—and one that is beginning to cause a lot of bankruptcies—is the interest-only mortgage. These loans don't amortize. You only pay interest, not principal. In theory, this lets you squeeze into an even more expensive house for a monthly payment you can afford. This is a particularly bad idea when placed in the wrong hands. The loans are not interest-only forever, after all. What happens when the interest is added to the payment you're already making? What if you're already paying the most you can afford? You don't need a calculator to figure out what happens next.

There have always been adjustable rate mortgages (ARMs). They amortize, and the initial interest rate is locked in at a low rate for a predetermined number of years. Then it re-adjusts. Again, if you're at or near your maximum monthly limit already when the interest rate adjusts, you may be in trouble if you haven't planned ahead. This includes taking into consideration if your income has gone down or if your expenses have gone up. The fact is adjustable interest-only mortgages don't allow you to plan very accurately. They are dangerous. This is why I recommend taking advantage of the system of checks and balances that having a team of advisors creates. Without consulting one another, would your accountant, financial planner, and lawyer agree such a loan is a good idea for you?

If you like the idea of buying and living in a house—if you can afford the taxes, insurance, and upkeep—then by all means, buy one. By owning a home, I don't mean living in the *bank's home*. Figure out how to pay it off as soon as you can. I'm no fan of borrowing against your house to put money in the stock market, by the way. Some people argue that money you send to a bank is money you'll never see again and that you ought to do a lot more with your equity. They don't talk much about risk, though. A paid off house gives you something to come home to. A failed stock portfolio does not. So let's talk a little more about investing.

OFF TO THE STOCKS WITH YOU (AN UNKNOWN PILGRIM MAGISTRATE)

ACT 4: No asset class has historically offered the long-term returns of common stocks.* Stocks are liquid: you can sell them any business day, and a buyer is almost always available. You can pay someone else to buy and sell stocks for you, or you can get yourself a computer and go for it. Some stocks pay dividends. Some offer the potential for growth in the future. Some don't ever seem to do much of anything.

A common stock represents ownership in a corporation. Your share is something you can buy or sell to other people who want to own your piece of

---

* More from the wacky compliance nuts: Past performance does not guarantee future performance.

185

this company. As I said before, the only reason to buy a stock is that you think someone else will buy it from you later, hopefully at a higher price. For all of the schools of thought on stock buying, it comes down to this: you buy a stock because you think you know something that no one else does. You hope, when everyone figures out what you know, that they will then pay up and buy your stock from you at a profit. It really is that simple.

Here's something to keep in mind: people can and do lose money on stocks. It is difficult to understand this concept in an age when stocks have done so well for so long. There is no FDIC insurance on stocks. As my hero Jimmy Buffet sings, "There is no dumbass vaccine." Teaching yourself how to invest can be a very expensive endeavor.

No matter what the guy on the infomercial tells you, there is no foolproof system that takes the risk out of investing. If someone had one of these methods, he'd be rich and retired, not teaching it at the Holiday Inn on Sunday afternoons. Besides, if his system worked so well, everyone would be doing it and then it wouldn't work anymore. Remember that whole supply and demand thing? The minute all of the students from the last 150 *How to Beat the Market* weekend classes got a signal from the lunar eclipse and entered their buy orders at the same time, the price of the stock they all wanted to buy would go up and, *Bada Bing*, the formula doesn't work anymore…

Sure, there are historical methods of tracking stock prices that seem to work some of the time, but some days, no matter what some "indicator" says a stock should do, it won't do it. Markets are funny that way. Stocks represent ownership in a company, not greyhounds on a racetrack. Successful investors buy companies at good prices. They have patience, a long-term economic outlook, and are willing to wait for others to recognize the value they perceive. Buying stocks should be an investment process, not a speculative one. If you buy a stock because you believe the company it represents has good management, has new products coming along that will be a big hit, has an unassailable position in its industry, or will grow faster than its competitors and earn more profit, you are thinking like an investor. If you are buying it because you think it might get taken over tomorrow by a consortium of Namibian banks, you are speculating. There are very wealthy speculators out there, and there are hundreds of broke speculators for every successful one. I like to think stock speculation is closer to betting at the dog track than it is to investing. I don't believe you should make a stock investment unless you are prepared to hold it for a number of years. You buy a stock as if you were buying the company itself. Imagine you had the resources to buy an entire company—which one would you buy?

GET A GOOSE THAT LAYS GOLDEN EGGS

ACT 5: In my mind, financial independence is within most people's grasp. I've met people from all walks of life and various income levels who have reached the point where their money will take care of them because they have taken care of their money. Getting there is not easy, otherwise everyone would have done it. But it can be done. Farrah Gray, the author of the book *Reallionaire*, is a product of Chicago's toughest projects. He made himself a millionaire by the age of 14. You can do it in America. You just have to put your mind to it. In *The Millionaire Next Door*, Dr. Thomas Stanley illustrated the characteristics of millionaires. You might be surprised about who they are and what they do. They aren't the jet-setting Hollywood stars. They are people living in your town in modest (paid-for) homes. They drive Ford F150 pickups and they live by a budget. They worry about their money and they take good care of it.

The Nestegg concept is best thought of as the Hotel California. You know, "You can check out anytime you like, but you can never leave." In my model, the money you save in your nestegg is *gone*, as if you blew it on Gatorade and pizza. You can't have it back. Now this requires a bit of discipline. The money you place in your nestegg is not to be touched—not even a little. Re-invest your earnings and get used to living below your means. Keep living on your current income and add to your nestegg regularly. You can use your 401K or your IRA for part of your plan, but be sure to save some money outside of your retirement plans too. Remember the 10 percent solution: pay 10 percent to your nestegg before you pay anyone else. This is common sense: if you want to make a sacrifice for your art, start here. Kick some money into the pot every month, skip some lattes, and get with the Affluent Artist™ program. Your goal is a lofty one—you want to become artistically and financially independent—so this is something you should feel a calling to. A little investing and goal-setting will go a long way.

How do you know when your nestegg is big enough to support you? That's a personal call, depending on your lifestyle and expenses. I think five percent is a good number to play with. In other words, can you live on five percent of the value of your nestegg annually? It's a good number to use because historical market returns tell us that you can withdraw five percent and still see some growth in your portfolio.

These are big numbers we are talking about here. I don't want you to get discouraged. The more you focus on your goal, the closer you'll get. Making some smart investments along the way will help you get there. Starting young helps too. Are you locked into this concept for life? I'd like to think so. Once you get excited about getting to financial independence, I think you'll be hard to stop.

Does all of this make you feel less creative, too structured? Release that. All I'm asking you to do is live on a little less than you make, no matter how much or how little that is. The alternative is worse. How unstructured will you feel if you stay broke all of your life? We're talking about getting Financial

Independence (you know freedom, the opposite of too structured). I'm asking you to do some stuff you hate, in small bites, so you can do more of the stuff you love, kind of like eating oysters… (Do you really believe that oysters help you… never mind).

If you start this process, you will have one ally that is one of the wonders of modern time, something that has been called man's greatest invention.

VERY INTERESTING

ACT 6: Remember how the bank made all that extra money on interest for your mortgage while you were paying back so little principal? That was because of the mathematics of compound interest. As an investor, compound interest plays for your team. Here's a useless historical fact from Wikipedia® to illustrate the potency of compound interest:

> If the Native American tribe that accepted goods worth 60 guilders for the sale of Manhattan in 1626 had invested the money in a Dutch bank at 6.5% interest, compounded annually, then in 2005 their investment would be worth over €700 billion (around USD $1,000 billion), more than the assessed value of the real estate in all five boroughs of New York City. [1*]

So, we are left to assume that the Native Americans didn't know about compound interest. They weren't alone. Here's how it works: you borrow five

---

1 * Wikipedia contributors, "Compound interest," Wikipedia, The Free Encyclopedia, http://en.wikipedia.org/w/index.php?title=Compound_interest&oldid=198033551 (accessed March 13, 2008).

large ($5000) on Sunday from my friend Vito to bet on this week's Bears game. Vito tells you the vig (that's the interest rate) is ten percent a day. You think, "Hey, no big deal!" You already owe him $5500 on Monday when the Bears tank, so you have to borrow from the kid's college fund to play tonight's game and you score. "What a relief!" Not so fast: you go to pay Vito $6000 on Tuesday, you know $500 a day, right? Wrong! Vito wants interest on his interest! So, you owe him $6050. If you don't get it to him today, he'll want $6,650 tomorrow or… well, you don't want to know. Fuhgetaboutit. Just pay him!

Vito makes interest on the interest. So can you as an investor. (It's legal, and you don't need a baseball bat to do it!) Getting a good investment return gets easier because, like they always told you, it takes money to make money. A $100,000 investment that compounds at 10 percent for five years does not grow to $150,000, as you might expect. (You know, $10,000 a year for five years.). With your interest earning interest, it actually grows to $161,051 dollars. Extending our example to 20 years gets us $672,745!

This also makes earning a good rate of return very, very important. If you drop the interest rate from 10 percent to six in the example above, that $672,745 only became $320,713. Now, the Wall Street guys are going to laugh pretty hard at this simplified explanation, but this is all you need to know. Sure, what I call interest is often called by names like dividends, earnings, appreciation, interest payments… whatever! The point is, when you get your money working for you, avoid the temptation to tap into it and let it go for as long as you can. On this, the Wall Street guys and I agree. We professional investment types have a complex financial expression we use to describe compound interest: "It doesn't suck!"

Prudence is Not Just a Girl's Name

So why not just shoot for the highest possible rate of return and forget about everything else? Well, that comes back to that supply and demand deal: the greater the potential return, the greater the potential risk. As risk rises, demand for the investment vehicle goes down. That's why they're willing to pay more for your money. That's right: some investments are riskier than others. Let's think of investments on a 1 to 10 scale. One is a treasury bill from the U.S. Government that is due today, no risk at all. Ten is a 100 million dollar lottery ticket for a lottery being held next year in Iran. Probably a little more risk than you should assume. Somewhere on that scale lie your investments. The trick is to know where. It's my scale, so I'm going to say that a house in the suburbs is a 5. It probably will go up in value, but there is no guarantee that it will. A good blue chip common stock is probably a five too. Most people, at least when they are getting started, should stay between 3 and 7 on my risk scale.

The Biggest Risk

Believe it or not, the danger for many people, especially in their retirement plans, is that they are too conservative and don't take full advantage of the benefits of compound interest over time. Way too much 401(k) money is invested in the guaranteed, lowest yielding options in the plan, especially for younger people. Suppose you faithfully invested $300 a month in your 401(k) for all 40 years of your career. The amount of return you achieve will have a tremendous bearing on your standard of living in retirement. Joe, who invests

---

*Those great people in the legal department wanted me to tell you that diversification does not guarantee a profit or protect against a loss. This is a hypothetical illustration and is not intended to reflect the actual performance of any particular security.

196 **PART THREE** Financial Stuff You Just Gotta Know

in the safest option and averages a three percent return for 40 years, has only about $275,000 in his retirement plan. Teresa, who used an asset allocation approach among several categories of investments and earns an 8.5 percent return, has a portfolio worth more than one million dollars. They invested the same amount of money in the same time span, but Teresa was rewarded for taking on more risk.*

Risk is not a bad word, as long as you understand what your risk is all about. Having a rudimentary knowledge of the investment options in your 401(k) is one of the most important steps you can take toward financial independence. Current research has shown that owning several different types of investments in your portfolio, distributed among different asset classes, is the most efficient way to combine safety and achieving higher returns. This is what professionals call asset allocation. If you own some growth stocks, some international stocks, some bonds, and some real estate you have theoretically diversified away some of your risk through asset allocation. Meet with your H.R. people or your investment professional about your 401(k) to discuss your personal asset allocation.

So how do you know where to invest, when to invest, and when to make changes? Knowing who to talk to about risk and your investment options is not something to talk about with the other waiters on your shift. I strongly advise forming a team of experts to help you through the ball of financial confusion.

HUNT IN PACKS

ACT 7: If miniature poodles came from the same ancestors as wolves, then some poor wooly mammoth was once hunted down and killed by a pack of little circus dogs, dying from a thousand small bites and terminal humiliation. I don't know why I felt the need to tell you this—it was on my mind, I guess. Oh, the importance of teamwork is where I was going, but who cut the poodles' hair anyway? Was it the cavemen? Did cave girls give them little bronze ribbons? Where did they get poodle clippers, anyway?

I've mentioned this before, but it bears repeating: you can't do it all. You can't be really good at your career, be creative, have a personal life, groom your poodle, and master all of this finance stuff by reading a few Internet articles. Something has to give, and I vote you leave the financial stuff to us professionals. Don't bring us the poodles!

And...I'm back. There are a lot of really good reasons to get some help with your money, not the least of which is an extra set of eyes will help you weed out the really bad ideas that cross your creative mind. Don't get me wrong— I've been investing for decades, and I still have the occasional really bad idea.

Sometimes just thinking about how I'd explain it to a client is all I need to snap me back to reality. There is no shortage of bad investment ideas out there, so you need to have a few good, sound fundamental ideas and pretty much stick with them.

Professional investment people come in all shapes and sizes. There's the insurance agent, the bank investment guy, the financial advisor from the big firm, the accountant who sells mutual funds and the Certified Financial Planner™. As I've mentioned before, my orientation is as a CFP® but I'm not going to tell you that not every one of us is a great fit for you. Your investment professional must meet at least three criteria: you have to like him, you have to trust him, and he has to be someone who is set up to help you.

The first two criteria are self evident. People sometimes use expediency as their first criteria for selecting a planner, ("He was working in the bank lobby," or "He does my plumbing too, so I already knew him!") or get intimidated into working with someone. If you aren't a financial type, all those leather chairs, walnut bookcases, and computers in the brokerage firm lobby can scare the crap out of you. Don't end up with someone who talks down to you, can't explain things to your satisfaction, or who won't let you finish a sentence. It is crucial that you find someone who you can tell your money secrets to. They will end up knowing more about you than your family members. And please, if your gut tells you that you're getting an old fashioned sales pitch, call a timeout. There *is never* a reason to make an investment that you don't understand or want or need.

The last part, finding someone who is set up to take care of you, is important. Just as lawyers can have vastly different practices—some practice real estate law, some do medical malpractice, and some specialize in contracts—financial guys also specialize. Some of us are planners, some are registered reps, and some are agents. Some of us prefer to deal with retirees and others work with Boomers. Some planners have functional specialties, such as estate or retirement planning. Some of us work on commission, some on a fee basis, and some for a percentage of assets. You might want to ask this up front. You also don't really want to be someone's smallest or even biggest client. Find a professional who is comfortable (or thrilled) to be working with someone just like you.

A good financial advisor will listen to your concerns, help define your goals, recommend an investment strategy, and educate you so that you can sleep at night. He should understand your risk tolerance and guide you to investments that are appropriate for you. He should be accessible: he should return your calls and send you legible statements. He should be able to recommend changes that are most appropriate for your life situation, tax status, and the changing economic outlook. He should never over-trade your account.

I believe strongly in a checks-and-balances approach to personal finance. My recommendation is that you hire an accountant to work with your financial guy. Depending upon your career path, you'll need to bring in other team members, such as lawyers, bankers and insurance agents but it's a good idea to let your team captain, (either your planner or your CPA) talk with your new people to make sure you are all on the same page. It's a good idea to let the insurance agent, for example, know why you need insurance coverage and how it fits in with everything else. So learn a lesson from those Darwinian superheroes, the poodles: always look your best and hunt in packs.

INSURANCE? WE DON'T NEED NO STINKING INSURANCE!

ACT 8: I know an artist who has a really cool job. In fact, he's famous in his field and people love to ask him all kinds of questions about his work. So when my friend gets on a plane and doesn't feel like talking, he'll tell someone that he sells insurance and usually this gets him a very quiet flight. If being an artist involves letting your inner child out to play, being an insurance agent pretty much involves locking your inner child under the basement stairs and threatening him with kitchen shears. So let's talk about the insurance you have to have. I'll make it as painless as I can because if you think reading about insurance is boring, you ought to try writing about it!

Health Insurance: Until we come up with a workable national health care system, you are going to have to get your own. I mean it—you really *have to get* *your own.* A simple operation can cripple you financially for life, and if you miss some kind of elective surgery because you can't afford it, you could be literally crippled for life. Many corporate jobs come with health benefits. In fact, that's why many people take corporate jobs. Please, don't risk going without this one. It amazes me when I meet someone who goes without health coverage.

Life Insurance: You don't buy it for yourself, since you won't be around to use the benefits. You really only buy life insurance to protect your loved ones or your business partners. My orientation is that life insurance is not a great investment or savings plan, but it does a very good job doing what it's supposed to do: *send a really big check to your survivors.* Most people don't have enough insurance and that is usually a result of not paying attention. Term insurance has gotten very inexpensive in today's Internet-driven marketplace. This type of insurance means you don't have any cash value, just death protection. You can lock in coverage and cost for a term of 10, 20 or 30 years. There are calculators available to figure out how much to buy. You usually want to replace your income and pay off your bills. The biggest drawback to term insurance is that you might outlive the coverage and not qualify for new coverage because of health conditions. This is worth talking about with your CFP® in more detail.

P & C: Property and casualty insurance is to protect you from something horrible like an accident, an act of nature, or something worse (like lawyers). Some of it you have to have, like auto insurance if you have a car, and there are other kinds that you only acquire as you move up the career ladder. My best advice regarding this type of insurance is to get a high deductible. It will lower your premiums substantially. In the event that you do have to make a claim, you'll have to pay more. Statistics show that you probably won't have to make a claim, so go for the lower premium.

Long-Term Care: If you are very rich or very poor, you don't need to buy Long Term Care (LTC) Insurance. Rich people can "insure" themselves and poor people can go on Medicaid. Everyone else should look into LTC coverage because an extended period of Long Term Care following an accident or illness can wipe you and your finances out.

Disability Income: This is fairly expensive and hard to qualify for on your own. Many corporations offer this as a benefit and I recommend you buy all you can. Anyone can get sick or become disabled. It is nice to know that your paychecks will keep coming!

STUFF I DIDN'T PUT OTHER PLACES...

ACT 9: **Roth vs. Regular IRA:** I get this question a lot, so let me make it easy on you: do you want to pay the government now or later? A Roth IRA allows you to make a contribution with after-tax dollars. As long as you leave the money invested for more than five years (or the number of years it takes you to reach age 59 ½, whichever is longer), you can take it all out *tax free*. There are income limits to qualify for this type of IRA. A traditional IRA allows you to deduct the amount you contribute to an IRA from your taxable income right away and allows the money in the IRA to grow on a tax-deferred basis. You do have to withdraw money eventually as taxable income, however.

Tax Deferral: The benefit of a traditional IRA is based on income tax reduction. You get an immediate deduction for making a contribution, and the growth inside of the IRA is not taxed until it is withdrawn. We call this *tax deferral*. Remember that compound interest thing? Well, tax deferral works because the money you should have paid in taxes is, instead, still working for you. Over time, tax deferral is a powerful ally. 401K accounts, annuities, pension plans and IRA accounts are just some of the investments that take advantage of tax deferral. If you bought this great little growth stock with your IRA contribution and it grew to millions of dollars and then you sold it, you wouldn't have to worry about taxes until you actually began to withdraw money from your account. (Just think: if we didn't have income taxes to dodge, the only reason to invest would be to make money. Imagine that!)

Inheriting an IRA: This one is kind of specialized. If you (or someone you know) are about to inherit money from an IRA or a pension plan, this concept can save lots o' money. A while ago, if you inherited an IRA (from someone other than your spouse), you had to cash the whole thing in within 5 years. Since IRA rollover accounts can contain lots of money, you were taxed on this windfall in a potentially high tax bracket. You could lose almost half of your money to taxes.

The tax laws have changed and now we've come up with something called a "stretch IRA". It works like this: Dad leaves his IRA to Junior, age 40. Junior *can* cash the whole thing in. Since he is a successful physician, he doesn't really need the money right now. Instead, he elects to "stretch" Dad's IRA out over his lifetime. He uses an IRA life expectancy table and takes out a very small percentage of the account this year and pays taxes on it. Each year he will have to withdraw an amount based on his life expectancy and the account value at the end of the year. This is a powerful tool that will allow him to make withdrawals while still letting the account grow on a tax deferred basis.

Income Tax Rates: You always hear stuff about "tax brackets." Let me give you a brief explanation of the concept. We have a "progressive" tax rate system, which means we all pay zero taxes on the first money we earn each year. Then, we are taxed at a fairly low rate on the next amount of money. Think of it like going up a flight of stairs. It's important, when planning, that you do your best to avoid stepping up into the highest brackets. That's why we are always looking to defer or avoid taxes anytime that we can.

What's an Annuity? Insurance companies are smart—that's why their skyscrapers are so big. Well, somehow, they have tricked the IRS into letting them have investments that grow tax deferred like IRA's and they call them annuities. These are like insurance policies that insure you against outliving your money. It works like this: you give an insurance company a big pile of money and they'll send you a check for the rest of your life, no matter how long you live. Some of the money that comes back to you in each check is your own principal.

There are some tax advantages when you "annuitize" your contract. Where the insurance companies outsmarted the IRS was when they said, "Look, sugar, we really are going to pay tax on this money someday, we promise, but let people invest money in the contract until they start taking checks. We'll call them deferred annuities because we'll defer the income. And since we are deferring the income, we'll defer the *taxes* until they take the income, okay?" And the IRS went along with it!

Now a whole class of assets called Tax Deferred Annuities is sold to investors everywhere. In practice, annuities can be good investments, but they tend to be oversold. There are few reasons to defer income if you are already retired, and in my opinion, there is almost no good reason to buy an annuity in an account that is already tax-deferred, like an IRA. Annuity contracts are designed to

*The Compliance Cops want me to tell you that you should find out if there will be state, local or AMT tax for your situation. GOD! I hate my job right now!!

be long term investments and there are often severe restrictions for getting at your own money early. Annuity contracts are a good thing to ask for a second opinion on if you're tempted to get into one.

Tax Free? Yes, it is possible to earn interest that is not tax deferred but tax free. That means you can get interest that you never, ever have to pay income tax on and, in most cases, tax free is even better than tax deferred. Municipal bonds, or "muni's", are government bonds that pay interest that is free of federal income tax. States, counties, municipalities, and other large entities offer these bonds to finance their operations. If you live in a state with a state income tax, income from your state's bonds is exempt. These bonds are a very popular place to store wealth and generate a monthly income.*

Credit Cards: Harder to get off than crack and more tempting than chocolate, credit card debt will keep you out of the game and on the bench longer than any other financial mistake you can make. I've talked about them at length. So here it is: you've just got to quit. I'm tempted to stop this chapter here, but I need to say a little more.

Here are some signs that you might just be in credit card trouble:
- Your cards are maxed and you are only sending in the minimum.

- You are spending more than 10% of your income to pay credit card bills.

- You are using one card to pay another in a frenzied attempt to borrow your way out of debt.

- You are paying for things like fast food lunches with credit cards because you don't have the money.

• People are calling asking if they can "help" you make a payment to their credit card company. By the way, a negative notation on your credit report lasts 7 years!

There is no pleasant way to stop an addiction and the folks at the credit card companies don't make it easy for you to quit. Everyday I get another credit card app in the mail or over the Internet. It takes a little discipline to remember that you do have to pay this money back some day. For most of us, it starts in college. Some studies say the average college student has an average of 4.7 credit cards.

If you are in trouble, talk with a good planner or non-profit credit counselor to work your way out. If you aren't, make this another sacrifice for your art, learn to pay cash, and pay off your balances each month. It might take a while, but you can this. I believe in you!

LEAVING A LEGACY

ACT 10: Making sure that your estate can help others is a noble gesture. The first thing you have to do to plan your estate is *have one*. The Starving Artist thing doesn't work here either. By setting up a will or trust before you pass on, you can insure that your assets go exactly where you want them to go: you may want your college or a museum or a family member to receive your assets, for example. Keep in mind that things like insurance policies, annuities, retirement plans and IRAs must have a named beneficiary. That money will not go through your will. They will pay directly to whomever you designate. You can designate your securities to pass in this manner too. Through a Transfer on Death account, your assets will pass to your beneficiary.

Many people will name a charity or their own trust as the beneficiary of a life insurance policy. Trusts or even your own foundation are excellent ways to direct your assets at death. They also protect your assets from probate and decrease any potential estate tax (essentially a death tax) that you might have to pay. Trust me when I tell you, there is A LOT more to know about estate planning. I recommend that you speak with a CFP® with an estate planning certificate.

No one says you have to die to give money away. My personal experience is that you get a lot more satisfaction if you give while living! Giving while you are alive can have the added benefit of providing an income tax deduction in exchange for your largess. For example, consider this year-end strategy: Suppose you had some stock that was worth $10,000. If you wanted to sell it and give the proceeds to your church, you'd have to pay taxes on the stock's appreciation. Here's a better technique: give the stock to your church—instead of the money—and let *them* sell it. The church won't have to pay any capital gains taxes and you will get to deduct $10,000 for income tax purposes.

In effect, you donated your $5,000 investment and got a $10,000 deduction. Let me tell you, this is not the way to do it if the numbers are reversed. If you bought the stock for $10,000 and it's now worth $5,000, *don't donate it!* Sell it first, so you can claim the $5,000 capital loss and then take the $5,000 deduction for the donation. If you donate the stock, you won't be able to claim the loss. Gifting appreciated assets works with most anything that can be readily sold by your charity from securities to art and even real estate.

No one here gets out alive. Just as you can leave an artistic legacy, you might also be able to leave a financial one. With a little planning, most estates can be settled with love and the wishes of the deceased observed. Many artists have left small and large contributions to help other artists. I don't see why you shouldn't think about it too. In effect this lets the creative energy that gave you your career live forever.

CONCLUSION:

THE AFFLUENT ARTIST™ METHOD

SO HERE'S WHAT I WANT YOU TO DO: Sidle up to that good lucking guy at the bar and see if he'll buy you a drink. Your hair looks fine, go ahead! He's got those Richard Branson teeth, the wavy blonde hair, the Hawaiian shirt and sandals, a Rolex. He just tipped the bartender $20 for a beer. His name is Financial Well Being and he is a good guy to know, a really good guy to know. He can open doors for you! If you get him working for you, you'll be more creative. You'll live more comfortably, and you'll be able to make a bigger difference in the world. He's really open to making new friends, but he has high standards. He really likes to hang with motivated people who don't give up easily. Here's what you'll have to do to hang with him:

Focus: Meditation and visualization work to help me get clear about things. Prayer might work for you, or maybe a long walk on the beach. Maybe you can just start writing and see where it goes. You need to get a picture of what you want from life. I'm not talking about setting goals (yet), I'm suggesting that you need to figure out your real life purpose. Nobody can give you this one. You're going to have to make your own decision about the purpose for your existence. Start here:

You know you have a talent and that you are creative. I'm suggesting that you line that up with your spirituality and incorporate your art into your life purpose. Don't fight it anymore. If you tried to abandon art but keep coming back to it, then embrace it. You are being sent these creative impulses for a reason—be open to them. The Universe is telling you something. I don't believe that the message is to starve and create: the same wealth building tools are open to you as an artist as they are to anyone, maybe more!

I meditate every morning. I use something called Holosync Technology (from Bill Harris of Centerpointe Research: h**ttp://www.centerpointe.com**) to get there. I focus on how my work that day will help me towards my life's purpose. This helps to keep me calm and focused. Finding your life's purpose is one of the reasons you were put here in the first place. I can't answer this one for you, but we both know it must include your art.

Set a Goal: Everyone's goal should be Financial Independence—the Holy Grail of Affluent Artistdom—but I think you need to begin with a short- and then an intermediate- term goal. A major problem with goal setting is that too many people use their own goals against themselves. They want to run a four minute mile by next week, become a millionaire by the end of the year, or lose 50 pounds between Thanksgiving and Christmas. In other words, they set unattainable goals and then beat themselves up when they don't achieve them. This self-help stuff won't work so well if you end up feeling like more of a failure than when you began. I really want you to select achievable goals at first and get used to small victories while you build some momentum.

Your short term goal might be something as simple as to get a job, make plans to get a job, or to quit smoking reefer long enough to think about making a plan to get a job—whatever. Make it something you can do in the next week. All you want to do is get the ball rolling. It will pick up more momentum if you are making and keeping promises to yourself. By the way, once you write this goal down, move heaven and earth if you have to in order to accomplish it.

Whatever you select, remember that you are testing yourself here: your brain is paying attention to see if you mean it this time. My wife and I have this great ritual when we decide to paint a room or add something to the garden. We love to go to the home center and buy all the stuff we need to do the job. Then, the job takes a while to actually get underway. Sometimes it's more fun to plan than it is to do. As you are building up speed, start with baby steps if necessary. The Universe respects action. Positive energy seems to attract more positive energy. Very often, starting work on something yields results in a completely different area than you planned. That's okay, go with it!

The intermediate goal needs to be made at the same time as the initial goal and is usually contingent on the first one being completed. If your long-term goal is financial independence, and your intermediate goal is to write a book, then your immediate step will be to do an outline. After that's accomplished you complete daily immediate steps to get you toward your intermediate goal until you've accomplished it. You know: one day at a time, one step at a time, right? Just do something every day that gets you going and continues to build momentum. Do something toward your goal every day, even Sunday, to keep it at the front of your mind (I recommend 5 things a day!).

I know many people get bogged down in this stage. They have too much going on in life, so many ideas, and are so busy that they don't accomplish anything at all. I really believe that there is a lot to be said for single-mindedness and dogged determination. Do something every single day to get you closer to your goal and don't go to bed until you do. If you are doing things that get in the way of your goals, then you are either not serious about your goals or you've set the wrong ones. Wanting to do too many things is dangerous. Your goal should be challenging enough to require you to stretch a little. It should take a lot of your energy.

You'll find that doing this every day will help you create successful habits, and successful people do all of the things that make them successful. They don't stop to consider that they are making sacrifices. Instead, they are so focused that it doesn't really occur to them that they could be having a few with the boys, or shopping with the girls.

If you've found that motivation, something that you can be single minded and determined about, then I applaud you. In fact, I love you! Motivated, creative people are my favorite. You have an energy about you that is attractive and infectious. People want to help you, and things happen because of your determination. People will want to work with you because they'll sense you are striving for greatness. They'll want to attach their stars to yours.

While you are making things happen, while you are setting and keeping goals, would it kill you to set a few intermediate money goals? I'm just saying… could you work in a little "I'm going to put $100 in my account this week," or "I want to pay off my credit card by the end of next month," while you're at it? Sure you can. Just raise your money consciousness a little and get those balls rolling too.

Here's the thing: if your art is keeping you from holding a real job, if money is really a problem, I believe you need yet another goal. This goal is to avoid the starving artist trap. Don't wait tables or drive a school bus. Find a career for yourself that works. Become a personal trainer, teach music, create an Internet-based copywriting service, do something that will support you financially while you wait for your big artistic break. This might require a change in some of your habits and self-limiting beliefs. Let's face it: you can do something to improve your situation.

If your long-term goal is financial independence, you'll need to get in the habit of saving and investing. As you get close to your artistic goals, you should be making financial planning goals too. If your art is being done on commission, plan to put some away. If you are working for a company, make a 401(k) contribution. Incorporate your finances with your life purpose. They really will work together!

Take Inventory: This one will be real easy for some of you, and it might take a while for others. You really need to know two things: What do I run on, and what do I have? This is only common sense: if you want to drive to Kansas, it would help to know which body of water you are dipping your toe into now. Let's figure out where you are, even though we know it's not where you plan to end up. You can go buy a fancy computer program for this one, but lined notebook paper is fine. You'll need two pages.

Page one is an income sheet. On the left side, list all of the money that is coming in. If you have a job paying you $250 a week, then that's all you list: Job $250. If you have trust fund income, business dividends, or child support, list them here as well. On the right hand side, list everything going out (and you really need to list everything: Rent $400, Dog Food $50, Dog Grooming $100, Dog Sweaters $45, Vet $75, Dog for Sale Ad $55 etc.) As painful as this is, it will help you get a sense of what can be cut out and what you need to give up to start putting money away. Be honest with yourself here. You just have to know some of these numbers if you want to get anywhere financially. If you have $1300 a month coming in and you are spending $1350 a month, you can't set many financial goals.

Page two is simply an inventory. List anything that you own by way of investments or savings. List your house's current market value and the balance of your 401(k), your IRA, and your checking account. On the other side, list what you owe: car loan, mortgage, etc. All you want is an honest assessment of where you are. Give yourself a break, you are starting the ball rolling. Don't worry if you aren't where you need to be. Page one examines your cash flow, and page two is a net worth statement.

That's it. I just want you to start being aware of money and start directing your thoughts toward accumulating more. Honestly, if you don't do these two pages, you've wasted a lot of time on this book. You aren't going anywhere without this step. The more you resist this one, the more you probably need to do it. Don't say, "Well, some people might need to keep track of their money, but I don't." Let me tell you something important: very few people who don't know what their cash flow and balance sheets look like are able to accumulate or hold onto wealth.

Live Below Your Means: Now that you know where you are and have a pretty good idea where you'd like to be, what are you willing to sacrifice for your art? "Everything," is not a good answer. Some income and some material stuff can probably help you get where you'd like to go faster. A job in a corporation might not allow you to produce what you are called to create, but the paychecks, benefits, and maybe even the contacts might help you to produce your art on the weekend or find the job you really want. Having a garage in which to write or paint might make it worth going to work during the day. Then there's that whole eating thing—you've probably got to do it too.

Why not begin here: Spend less money. That's all, just don't buy as much stuff and don't eat out as much. Go to the library instead of the bookstore. Make your long distance calls after 7:00, and carry lunch to work. This doesn't just apply to young, starving artists. It applies to you Corporate and Self-Employed artists too. I'm in the foxholes on this one, serving on the front lines, and I talk to people about their money every day. Usually the conversation goes pretty well if we are talking about saving money and retiring and if I'm showing all kinds of rosy predictions about their future. But, as soon as I ask, "What are you going to give up to save more money?" the warm fuzziness ends and people get very uncomfortable. They can't imagine giving anything up or going without any of their comforts.

The majority of middle class Americans I see have money in their home equity and in their 401(k) and that's it. They don't have any other savings because they don't have a mechanism to save. The 401(k) money comes out of their paycheck and their home equity builds up because they make their mortgage payments. Saving money is not cool. It's not even a consideration. Most people live paycheck to paycheck because they live above their means. This is a *choice*. Our Constitution does not say that we must all die broke, and no law says we are obligated to use credit cards. Americans have decided that they have to have it all and they have to have it now.

So if you want your friends to think you are really different, get good with money! They'll think you are very eccentric if you drive a used car, pay cash for stuff, and brown bag your lunch. Use the inventory sheets we designed in the last step to help you figure out what you *can* put away, then put it away and leave it alone! This sacrifice for your art will eventually give you the freedom to follow your muse, to be your own patron. Besides, less time at the mall will give you more time in the studio!

Debt: In the Affluent Artist™ system, credit cards are only recommended for convenience. You need to pay off your balances every month or admit to yourself that you actually can't afford to purchase an item. You are allowed to say no to yourself once in a while. It's kind of liberating when you realize that if you don't take control of your debt you don't have any chance of taking care of your finances. Your cards can get out of control in a hurry and our system recommends you *pay them, close them, and shred them.*

Systematic Savings: My professional observation is that people who have real wealth have it because they take care of their money and they probably started at an early age. We use the ten percent figure because it's a nice round number. I don't care if you save $5 a week: you have to get in the habit of doing it every time you get money. Not only do you have to *make* yourself save at first, you have to take pride in it. Congratulate yourself for being good with money and then do it again! If you can convince yourself to be enthusiastic about beginning to accumulate a nest egg, you have taken the biggest step. You are really on your way.

Where to invest is almost not important. It's the *when* that matters at first. Set up an automatic withdrawal from your checking account or from your paycheck. That way you make sure you pay yourself before anyone else. Not seeing the money at all is a good way to go. You'll find that you don't miss what you never have. As the money grows, asset allocation and investment selection become very important indeed. I recommend that you begin with securities, probably mutual funds because of their diversification and relative liquidity. Avoid the impulse to go for the big score. Be patient. It's the get rich slowly approach that we're going for.

Nurture and Grow Your Artist: If you are waiting tables while trying to get your break, working as a Corporate Artist running a design firm, or searching the world for your next great production, you have a responsibility to nurture your creativity. The variety of Starving Artist who has become such a passionate businessman that he forgets he is an artist is not hard to find. You start off as a great designer and before you know it, you are a manager. Suddenly you're worried about personnel, payroll, scheduling vacation time, and budgets instead of about art. It's a good idea to remember what you brought to the party and don't lose yourself in all of the business stuff.

I suggest that one of your goals every month is to find time to nurture your inner artist. Take a class, a tele-seminar, or a tour of Italy…do something to remind yourself that you are first and foremost an artist. Remind yourself that creativity implies creation. Your unique vision, your gift, is ultimately what people pay you for, so you can't afford to get too bogged down in the money stuff. There are people out there who will be much better at spreadsheets than you, so go with your passion.

Passion is required, as you know. My personal experience is that artists without passion are not very fun to be around. If your work doesn't excite you, then find an outlet after work. If your work makes that impossible, *quit!* Life is too short to be lived without joy and enthusiasm. You need to be very careful to avoid letting your career path take a turn into the land of the bored and disturbed. Jobs may come and go, but your gift needs to be nurtured.

Hire Your Team: If you are willing to remain an artist, and one who pays attention to money, you need to hire some people. I've already talked about this at length. I believe that a Certified Financial Planner™ is a very good person with whom you could strike up a relationship. Having someone who can provide a little momentum to your financial plan—someone with a little accountability—is probably all you need to get going. As your wealth increases and your fame spreads, having a reliable financial guy who brings his expertise to the table might be just the ticket to keep you out of trouble.

Things happen: the movie deal comes in, you sell your script, or you find yourself on the cover of a magazine. You'll find that spectacularly bad investment opportunities will appear at your doorstep every day. A good financial planner will act as a filter, someone who can help you make the right decision. Be sure that all your investment decisions are still your decisions. As I've said before, I don't recommend giving anyone discretion over your money. You should stay involved and find advisors who respect your wishes to do so.

I am a big fan of checks and balances. I suggest your second team member be a good tax accountant. Not just someone at the mall who prepares tax returns, but a real Certified Public Accountant (CPA) who can help you with other financial decisions. In the Affluent Artist™ system, your CPA is also a filter for investments and overall strategy as well as a backup to your financial CFP®. This is never someone who tries to actually sell you investments. As your wealth increases, he becomes a very important resource to help you pay the least amount of tax possible. Your CFP® and your CPA should know each other and be able communicate with each other. They should not work together. I think they ought to act as checks and balances against one another. Mistakes and misjudgments can be made by even the most well-meaning financial professionals. As a professional, I like the idea of having someone looking over my shoulder. I think it helps everyone involved in the process, especially my client.

Other team members might come and go. You bring them in as you need them. Insurance agents, attorneys, book agents, realtors, mortgage brokers, and the like are all valuable when you need them. The trick is to find one who specializes in what you need for each job. Your team leaders—the CFP® and the CPA—are probably in a network that includes these other professionals. They can help guide you to the right person when the time comes. As your career progresses, you'll have to employ a variety of specialists. Make sure that you are always in charge and that you make the final decisions.

Network: Even in today's global economy the world is still a pretty small place. Knowing a few people who know a few people can go a long way. If you have branded yourself as someone who can be trusted and has talent, word will get out. Being someone who can work and play well with others is a very special talent when it comes to creative people. Most people would rather work with the guy who *doesn't* show up late and high, even if he is a genius. So let people know you are available to help with projects. If you don't have something to offer on a particular project, make some calls and find someone who does. Putting people together is a talent all by itself. You might be surprised how much it helps you to make a few simple introductions.

Brand: Being known as a specialist can be a helpful tool in creating your brand. Identify a market for an aspect of your creative self and major in it. Become an answer to someone's search. Be the guy who has "just what I've been looking for" for enough people and you'll be on your way to becoming financially successful. You can break out into other products after your brand becomes well known.

Mentor: Ask for help. It has been my experience that people love to help others and are usually honored that someone would ask them. Often, the person being asked gains as much from mentoring as the person they're helping: seeing their world through a fresh set of eyes can often be just what the creative spirit needs. The sooner you accept that you don't *have to* learn every lesson the hardest way possible, the better off you'll be. So find a hero, someone who has done what you want to do, and ask questions about everything from creation to marketing and everything in between.

Life is funny. Someone will ask you for help too. You owe it to the Universe to enthusiastically jump in and share, just as the artists who guided me through this writing process did. Telling someone "Watch your money!" is especially good advice. You can't understate the things that can go wrong financially for an artist. A good way to mentor is to introduce them to the concepts you've learned here.

The Affluent Artist Dashboard™: You need to keep track of your money without obsessing over it. I recommend using something we call The Affluent Artist Dashboard™ to help you get in the right place. By paying attention to the big financial picture, you'll develop a money-consciousness that will become a natural and important part of your artistic career. Some financial types might recognize that the Dashboard is a very simple spreadsheet designed to help you monitor your weekly progress and provide accountability.

The rudimentary dashboard can be used by any artist, regardless of what financial stage you are currently visiting. Just use that inventory I told you to take a few minutes ago and list it like this:

AFFLUENT ARTIST DASHBOARD

My Bank Accounts	My Monthly Bills
My Investments	
My Monthly Income	My Nurturing Project
My Short Term Goal	
My Intermediate Goal	

The secret of the Dashboard is in its simplicity. Attended to weekly, the Dashboard provides accountability. It will help you keep track of your investments and your brain will begin to focus on your goals. This is a sneaky way to get in the habit of setting goals and working toward them, not to make you crazy or obsessive.

Just know that every Friday night, you have to write down a few numbers. Of course, you can do this anytime you want. I suggest you schedule your Dashboard time on your calendar and make it a date that cannot be changed. We are after accountability with this process.

Gathering your data should not be a real big deal. Just write down your deposit for your pay, keep track of things like rent, and know what you are working toward. Your short-term goal could be a money goal, like "save $100," or it can be something like "write three chapters." Your intermediate goal is the same. It could be to have a net worth of $250,000 or to have your Broadway debut. These two goals need to line up. Your short-term goal should be a step toward your intermediate goal. It's understood that your long-term goal is artistic and financial independence, so your intermediate goal needs to line you up on this path.

The nurturing goal is as important as the money goals. Every week you need to do something to improve yourself as a creative person. It might be to read a book, attend a class, or teach a new artist a skill you already have. It's crucial that you integrate money and your creative process, so we make nurturing your inner artist the most important component of the Dashboard.

I urge you to be creative with the Dashboard, to incorporate your art in the process. Use your medium to make it something that you enjoy looking at and working with. Be playful. Use humor and sarcasm if it works for you. Do whatever makes this tolerable. I'd love, by the way, to see a picture of your

Dashboard. Send it to the Affluent Artist™ website and we'll proudly display your work.

You can also add lines to the Dashboard, perhaps putting in a special goal such as paying off student loans or including income from the sale of a project. Keep it simple. If you get so caught up in this stuff that you need to keep detailed spreadsheets on personal financial software, go for it. Always boil the numbers down to a simple few lines that you can absorb with a glance. My fear is if completing the Dashboard becomes a more time consuming project than it needs to be, you'll put it off, dread it, or quit working on it altogether. Just as you only glance at the dash on your car to check your gauges, the only purpose of the Affluent Artist Dashboard™ is to help you keep track of what you are doing. Spending too much time playing with the gauges won't get you where you need to go. The Dashboard is designed to keep track of your progress. You're the one driving the car!

My hope is that you will not be afraid of writing a few numbers down once a week, that you'll allow money to become an ally in your artistic career. As you become more comfortable with money, you'll find that you can do some wonderful things for yourself, your family, and your art. I'd love to hear about your journey and your successes. Remember: the Universe has given you a special talent, and the world is waiting to share it. Please don't deprive us of your work!

ACKNOWLEDGEMENTS

I t is impossible to write a book without friends. It turns out that the lonely writer with a word processor is just part of the team and could no more put out a book alone than a quarterback could win the Rose Bowl without the rest of his squad. The new friends I made during the process, the old friends who helped more than I could imagine, and the support I received is indeed humbling and exciting at the same time. I had a posse all along, I just didn't know it!

The Affluent Artist™ would never have been born, it turns out, if Tanya Carpenter and Shayla Roberts didn't act as twin muses in August, 2007. They had the passion for the project and saw me as an artist before I even did. Their support and vision throughout the writing process was more valuable than they could know and their confidence in my inner artist was an inspiration. Jennifer Wilkov was introduced to me next and her consulting program helped me to find my voice and a publisher. Jennifer loves books and she has the talent to help you find your book and get it on paper.

My best friend, Keith Malick, opened his Rolodex® and his heart to me.

He encouraged me to go for it and many of the artists I interviewed were friends of his. Stewart Clark of Discovery Cove in Orlando seemed to see the possibilities of the Affluent Artist™ before I fully realized them and was especially encouraging. His bride, Kelly Flaherty Clark, graciously gave me a behind the scenes tour of SeaWorld and her dolphin show. She is the one who calls her creative colleagues "passionate people" and I happily stole the line.

Many of my friends that I met through my association with Jack Canfield's Breakthrough to Success Program helped me to believe in myself and the project, gave advice when I needed it, and even agreed to be interviewed. There are so many of them but I especially want to thank Robert MacPhee, Jesse Ianello, Laverne Gehman, Dr. Beth Erickson, Pete Winiarski, Barbara Reid, Brad Jaffe, Tomas Michaud, and Alan Milham. Of course Jack Canfield himself is living proof that kind, caring people can also become successful. He became a role model to me when I thought I was too old to have role models.

My Mastermind group of Ian Coles, Kathy Fields, Dr. Priya Balakrishnan, Steven and Kimberly Yurisich, and Dan Haynes offered great support and motivation.

Jackie Hoepfner, my assistant and office manager, not only keeps me grounded, she offers common sense and a good ear when I go too far off into Artist's Land to still be a good businessman. She is a good friend and colleague.

Thom Winckelmann is another good friend and a Ph.D. candidate who is a GREAT editor. I recommend you contact him through my office if you need someone who will "Edit for Food". He has a knack for preserving your voice and making you coherent. (No small task in the case of my writing!)

My children, Suzanne Istvan (and her husband Adam), Lizzy, Rachel and James DiBiasio always had great interest and encouragement for the project. Special thanks to my wife of twenty years, Teresa, for watching the transformation in me with patience and more than a little tolerance over the years. She married a stockbroker and ended up with an author, not the trip she signed up for but an interesting journey nonetheless.

To the Army of Angels who watch over me and my loved ones, Thank You.

Printed in the USA
CPSIA information can be obtained
at www.ICGtesting.com
JSHW012015140824
68134JS00025B/2425

9 781600 374784